D0065646

AFTER CHRISTMAS

HOW CHRIST'S BIRTH
CHANGED EVERYTHING

AFTER
CHRISTMAS

HOW CHRIST'S BIRTH
CHANGED EVERYTHING

JEREMY ROYAL HOWARD
+ DOUG POWELL

HOLMAN
REFERENCE

NASHVILLE, TENNESSEE

After Christmas: How Christ's Birth Changed Everything

© Copyright 2016 by Jeremy Royal Howard and Doug Powell

B&H Publishing Group
Nashville, Tennessee

ISBN 978-1-4336-4665-2

Dewey Decimal Classification: 234
Subject Heading: JESUS CHRIST—NATIVITY\GOSPEL\
SALVATION

Printed in China
1 2 3 4 5 6 7 8 9 10 • 21 20 19 18 17 16
DBS

CONTENTS

CHAPTER 1

THE PROBLEM

WHAT IS YOUR ALL-TIME FAVORITE CHRISTMAS GIFT? Whether you were a child or an adult, think about what made it so special. Was it something you had wanted for a long time? Something you just couldn't live without? Or was it one of those unanticipated gifts, one you never dreamed of having? Whatever it was and for whatever reason, the gift was perfect and you remember it to this day.

That favorite gift says something about you, but it says even more about the one who gave it. That person really knew you, understood your wants and needs. Far from a shot in the dark, they chose with precision and accuracy. They also gave of their time and resources, and they crafted a plan for presenting it to you. What it all means, of course, is that they cared for you. Their gift is the proof.

As much as we love receiving gifts, it's even more fulfilling to *give* them. How can that be? The one who dies with the most toys wins, right? No, that's not the key to happiness or any good end. Giving brings us more joy than receiving because giving reflects the character of God our Maker, the ultimate Gift Giver.

In this chapter we look at some of the great gifts God has given, what they say about both God and us, and how it all came under threat by a misdeed long ago.

AFTER CHRISTMAS

THE GIFT OF THE UNIVERSE

Do you know any artists? If so, you may have noticed that their work reflects their personality and message. Art is communication; to observe the art is to observe the artist.

The universe is the ultimate artwork. By observing it we can learn things about its Artist and his message (Psalm 19). God's message through nature comes to all people, whether or not they ever hold a Bible. One message from nature is that the universe—every part of it—depends on God for existence. It is made of temporary stuff and is destined to fade away. Creation arose, persists, and wanes by the will and purpose of God.

So what's the point of it all? God wasn't in need of anything. He had no lack or deficiency that drove him to make a world. His motivation was to share his abundance and glory for the enjoyment of others. This means the world is a gift, a kindness shown by a God, who wants to delight his creatures.

THE GIFT OF POWER

Once there was nothing aside from God. And then, by his Word, *a world*. Every atom, every planet, every bright and burning star—all of these erupted into existence because God said it should be so.

What do you call power like that? Theologians call it omnipotence (omni = all; potence = power). Omnipotence means God can do anything that is logically possible (he cannot make a square circle) and compatible with his character (he cannot sin). Speaking to God about God's power,

THE PROBLEM

Job put it this way: "I know that You can do anything and no plan of Yours can be thwarted" (Job 42:2).

One wonders, does a God so grand ever bother with us? You are one person among seven billion, and Earth is a tiny blue dot afloat in a vast sea of unknown worlds. You could be pardoned for thinking you don't matter to God, but the Bible insists otherwise. Psalm 121:3 says, "He will not allow your foot to slip; your Protector will not slumber." So attentive is God that he even knows the number of hairs on your head (Luke 12:7).

The God who spoke the world into existence cares for you, but some say God must contend with an uncooperative universe in hopes that his goals pan out. If that were true, God would be a sympathetic listener and a companion in the fray, but only sometimes would he be a savior. Too often he would fail, left to join us in picking up the pieces of a world gone wrong.

But that's not the God of the Bible. He created worlds with words, rules all according to his wisdom, and gives the gift of his power to answer our prayers and fulfill his purposes.

THE GIFT OF REASON

Genesis 1:26-27 says, "Then God said, 'Let Us make man in Our image, according to Our likeness . . .'"

> So God created man in His own image;
> He created him in the image of God;
> He created them male and female.

AFTER CHRISTMAS

Being made in God's image doesn't mean God has eyes, ears, a nose and mouth. Rather, it means that we have characteristics and abilities that resemble God's. We are "little *c*" creators, and we practice "little *s*" sovereignty over creation.

At the heart of this is the gift of reason. We are thinkers. The gift of thought allows us to weigh plans and actions and decide their moral value. Our actions are not dictated by instinct or logical necessity. Rather, they are the result of deliberation, and that's why we are held accountable. A tree that falls onto a car is not held blameworthy, for the tree lacks reason or willpower. However, a person cutting that tree down so that it will fall on the car is blameworthy because he has reason and willpower, and he has misused both.

We were given the gift of reason for good purposes. Life isn't just something that happens to us; by the use of our minds we can help shape a world that honors God and values life.

THE GIFT OF RELATIONSHIP

Perhaps the ultimate mark of God's image is our ability to form relationships. Personalities differ, but we all long to have fulfilling connections. It isn't good for man to be alone, and so God made us male and female (Genesis 2:18-25). Even more fundamentally, we are incomplete without God. Augustine wrote, "You have made us for yourself, and our hearts are restless until they rest in you."

Our hunger for relationship reflects God's nature. God is eternally one in divine substance and three in person (Father, Son, Spirit). God has never been alone, and neither should we be. Life is lived best when we give and receive the gift of relationship.

THE GIFT OF STEWARDSHIP

One way to exercise our gifts of reason and relationship is to care for the world and make it a better place. This is the gift of stewardship. God didn't create us to be idle and bored. He gave us fulfilling work to do. He told Adam and Eve, "Be fruitful, multiply, fill the earth, and subdue it. Rule the fish of the sea, the birds of the sky, and every creature that crawls on the earth" (Genesis 1:28). Taking the entire Bible into account, we see that we are responsible for more than just animals. We are to create culture and promote actions and values that advance human well-being. We harness natural resources and advance knowledge so that we may excel in the human craft. We also create art to weave connection, celebrate life, and express ourselves, just as God created, connected, and expressed himself in the great art that is this universe. The gift of stewardship gives us the purpose and dignity that are necessary to true fulfillment. It's a good gift of God, and without it we would be reasonable but lack a driving reason, relational but without life-giving relational investment in others.

THE GIFTS MISUSED

Adam and Eve were the pinnacles of creation. Fresh from the soil and gifted with so much privilege, they were set for trouble-free life. But they allowed doubt to enter their hearts. God had told them not to eat from the tree of the knowledge of good and evil (Genesis 2:17). The message was clear: eat of the tree and you will die. But they listened to a lesser voice. At the bidding of the serpent, they grasped after a lie (Genesis 3:6-7). The serpent—the tool of Satan in this sad event—was cast down into the dust for his deception, to be trodden upon and despised for the duration of the Earth age. For Adam and Eve there would now be pain and needless toil, unwelcome intrusions into a life designed for better things. But worse than this was death, both physical and spiritual. To ensure an eventual physical death, God cast Adam and Eve out of the garden so that they couldn't access the tree of life. As they left the garden, bowed low with shame, they understood that life was now measured, finite, progressing toward an *end*. Worse still, they walked this dark new path alone. Gone was the God who had once walked with them. He had withdrawn and fallen silent, the Creator hiding from creation.

Some complain that Genesis portrays God as storming off in a tantrum, but such thinking misses a central point: as holy and omnipotent Creator, God is perfect in all his attributes. He created humans to be his representatives on earth, bearers of his likeness. His standard for judging is himself, his own perfections. The thing about perfection is it's all or nothing. Something is either all the way perfect or else it doesn't share in perfection at all. More to the point, any hint of immorality is an infinite strike against the perfect and infinite morality of God.

The day that Adam and Eve were banished from the garden, we followed in their train. Each of us retraces their footsteps, but it's not just their example that leads us into error. We are born under the curse, outfitted with a marred nature that makes sin our native choice (Psalm 51:5). In this state, we aren't just spiritually feeble but spiritually *dead* (Ephesians 2:1). We're under sin, alienated from God, unable to please him (Romans 3:9-18). Any effort to wash away sin's stain by doing more good things than bad is wasted. We can't earn God's favor. Our good deeds are tainted with self-concern and pride, so lacking in substance that they all get blown away by the wind (Isaiah 64:6).

What's to be done? By us, *nothing.* The task is beyond us. We lie spiritually lifeless before God, a shell of what we were meant to be. If there's to be restoration, it must be by God's own choice, another and even more amazing gift from the Creator's hand.

REFLECT & DISCUSS

1. Think about your favorite Christmas gift. What made it so special? Describe the gift, its meaning, and the giver.

2. Read Psalm 19:1-6. How does creation reflect the glory of the Creator?

3. God notices you among the vast ocean of the universe. What circumstance in your life right now makes this especially important to you?

4. We are created for relationships, but many of them are in need of repair. What can you learn from the work of Jesus in his incarnation that could lead you in renewing a broken relationship?

5. How does the story of Adam and Eve's banishment from Eden help you better understand Christmas?

CHAPTER 2

THE PROMISE

WHEN ADAM AND EVE LEFT THE GARDEN, they essentially walked right out of Scripture. We're told next to nothing about them afterward. They had children, obviously, and one son murdered another (Genesis 4). Other than that, the Bible is silent. They had played their part, fouled up their role, and the human story moved on.

Possibly God never interacted with Adam and Eve again. Imagine the heavy silence. But he didn't send them off without hope. First, God showed his ongoing care by explaining their punishment and by clothing them (Genesis 3:16-21). More importantly, in his curse upon the serpent, God assured them that he would someday undo the ruinous impact of their rebellion. To the serpent, tool of Satan, God said:

I will put hostility between you and the woman,
and between your seed and her seed.
He will strike your head,
and you will strike his heel.

GENESIS 3:15

God is speaking in depth here. More than just a statement about humankind's contention with snakes, he's saying that he would send a Savior to defeat evil, and that the Savior would be extraordinary. He foretells that the Savior would come from the seed of *woman*. In human conception, it's the man who provides seed. By saying that someone will come from the seed of woman, God prophesied about the virgin birth of the Savior. The savior would be no mere son of man. And when he comes, God said, the Savior would be wounded by Satan ("you will strike his heel," a less than fatal wound), but ultimately would triumph ("He will strike your head," a fatal blow).

What We Learned While Waiting

Salvation is God's work; he accomplishes it in his way and in his time. Adam and Eve never met the Savior, nor would any of their descendants for many generations. God's reasons for unfolding salvation so gradually (as humans perceive it) are unknown to us, but through humanity's long wait one thing became clear: no man, no matter how righteous or wise or strong, could save us. Whether chosen for leadership by God or by the will of men, all merely human saviors failed.

Noah Could Not Save

With corruption seated in every heart, humans were destined to build corrupt societies. At some point in our early history, God looked throughout the world and saw every thought was "evil all the time" (Genesis 6:5). So abject was the problem that God said he regretted making humans (Genesis 6:6). This wasn't a confession of poor judgment by God, but a purposefully humanlike expression that signaled the depth of his displeasure at immorality. In the midst of this, though, there was a glimmer of hope.

A man named Noah "found favor in the sight of the LORD" (Genesis 6:8).

In a preview of the final and comprehensive judgment to come at the end of time, God drowned everyone except for Noah and his family (Genesis 6:17). But once Noah reestablished humanity's foothold on the earth, he proved that even *his* heart was corrupt (Genesis 9:20-28). The flood stalled the spread of evil for a time, but Noah was no basis for an improved humanity. Far from being a savior, Noah himself needed saving.

MOSES COULD NOT SAVE

Important as he was, Noah never wrote a scrap of Scripture. The first man God called to that task was Moses, a Hebrew who enjoyed Egyptian privilege as an adopted son of Pharaoh's household. God placed Moses in that position not so Moses could live a life of luxury, but so Moses could serve as champion of Hebrew emancipation. God did miraculous things through Moses, including delivering the Hebrews by parting the Red Sea (Exodus 14:21), feeding them meat and bread from heaven (Exodus 16), and guiding them by pillars of fire and cloud in the wilderness (Exodus 13:21).

Despite all of this, Moses didn't qualify as Savior. He couldn't even save himself. After his many triumphs, Moses failed in a simple task. He asked God to provide water for the people, who were complaining bitterly. As Provider, God was willing, and so he told Moses to speak to a rock so that water would come from it. It was to be yet another sign that God provides for his people, but Moses lost his temper and put the focus on himself. Instead of speaking to the rock, he *smashed* it. He was right to be fed up with the people, but by striking the rock, he robbed God of honor and the chance to reveal himself in his chosen way. As a result, God said, "Because you did not trust Me to show My holiness in the sight of the Israelites, you will not bring this assembly into the land I have given them" (Numbers 20:12).

If that seems unjust, it's because we've not fully grasped the standard of God's perfection. Any adequate mediator between God and humanity must be perfect, or else God has declared that his holy perfection doesn't matter after all, that sin is just a trifle. Moses was a righteous man used mightily by God, but we can be grateful that God ultimately rejected him as inadequate. What we need is an advocate who can stand before God and represent us faultlessly, to ensure that our sin debt is paid. Moses, a good man but flawed, stands alongside us in need of a perfect advocate.

Kings Could Not Save

Ideally the Hebrews would have chosen God as their king and not mimicked the nations, but impatience and unbelief drove them to demand a human king (1 Samuel 8:6-8). God accommodated them and gave them Saul, their first ruler and a harsh national lesson. Saul looked the part (1 Samuel 9:2), but looks can deceive. He was a disobedient mess from start to finish. For example, through the prophet Samuel, God told Saul to destroy completely the Amalekite people and their possessions (1 Samuel 15:3). Spare nothing and no one, God said, but Saul thought he knew better. He spared king Agag and took the best livestock. When Samuel asked Saul why he didn't obey God, Saul protested:

AFTER CHRISTMAS

> But I did obey the LORD! . . . I went on the mission
> the LORD gave me: I brought back Agag, king
> of Amalek, and I completely destroyed the
> Amalekites. The troops took sheep and cattle
> from the plunder—the best of what was set apart
> for destruction—to sacrifice to the LORD your God
> at Gilgal.
>
> 1 SAMUEL 15:20-21

Every sinner has a rationale for their disobedience, but it's always faulty. Saul's weak effort was no exception. Here's how God replied through Samuel:

> Does the LORD take pleasure in burnt offerings
> and sacrifices
> as much as in obeying the LORD?
> Look: to obey is better than sacrifice,
> to pay attention is better than the fat of rams.
> For rebellion is like the sin of divination,
> and defiance is like wickedness and idolatry.
> Because you have rejected the word of the LORD,
> He has rejected you as king.
>
> 1 SAMUEL 15:22-23

One hardly feels as badly for Saul as for Moses, but the same unshakable problem undermined both men: a sinful heart. The same was true of Israel's most famous king, Saul's successor, David. David was loyal to God, a man after God's own heart (1 Samuel 13:14), but he was also a man after Adam's heart. After defeating many enemies, overcoming incredible struggles, and expanding the kingdom, David had many reasons to obey God and trust him in all things. He lacked nothing. Yet he gave in to sin and not only committed adultery but compounded his error by murdering the husband in order to cover up the adultery. God, speaking through the prophet Nathan, convicted David, saying:

> I anointed you king over Israel, and I delivered you from the hand of Saul. I gave your master's house to you and your master's wives into your arms, and I gave you the house of Israel and Judah, and if that was not enough, I would have given you even more. Why then have you despised the command of the LORD by doing what I consider evil?
>
> 2 SAMUEL 12:7-9

King after king, prophet after prophet, all proved that their virtues were mixed with vices. Even David's son Solomon, deemed the wisest man ever to have lived, mistook God's gifts for signs of his own sufficiency. All the good men and all the evil men served ultimately as signposts pointing to the need for an ultimate Prophet and King.

THE PEOPLE COULD NOT SAVE THEMSELVES

The people proved that it wasn't just their spiritual and national leaders who were flawed and in need of a redeemer. As their history unfolded in the Old Testament, the Hebrews showed how being a part of Israel isn't what brings salvation. Salvation only comes through faith. But time and again they tried to make their own salvation. Even as they waited for Moses to bring the law down from Mount Sinai, they built a golden calf and named it after God (Exodus 32).

The failures of even righteous leaders were no surprise to God, for he used all of their failures to make clear that salvation must be a work of God. But how can God satisfy God's wrath against human sin when no mere human is righteous enough to represent us or strong enough to bear the penalty in our place? It goes back to the hint first given in Genesis 3:15. The one whom God would send—the Messiah—would be no mere human. God sprinkled hints of the Messiah's divine identity throughout Old Testament revelation. In fact the details are so abundant that one could almost say that the Old Testament contains a biography of Jesus. Examples include:

- born of a virgin (Isaiah 7:14)
- born in Bethlehem (Micah 5:2)
- rejected (Psalm 22:1)
- betrayed for 30 pieces of silver (Zechariah 11:12-13)
- pierced in hands and feet (Psalm 22:16)
- died with thieves (Isaiah 53:12)
- buried in a rich man's tomb (Isaiah 53:9)
- raised from the dead (Psalm 16:10; Isaiah 53:10)

Altogether there are more than 60 prophecies about the Messiah in the Old Testament. The point of them all is to recognize the arrival of God in the flesh, the Savior who came to do what we could never do for ourselves.

THE PROMISE

REFLECT & DISCUSS

1. Describe a time when you had to wait for an answer from God.

2. What do we learn about ourselves from the account of Noah's faithfulness to God and his later failure?

3. Moses lost sight of the need to uphold God's holiness to the Hebrews. In what ways are you currently distracted from upholding God's holiness before a watching world?

4. We look for people of power to bring meaning, purpose, and healing into our lives. Why do we do that? How can this be misused? Describe how you can turn from false sources.

5. What does it tell us about God's character that he included so many prophecies about the Messiah in the Old Testament?

CHAPTER 3

THE FULFILLMENT

CHRISTMAS CARDS ENVISION JESUS'S BIRTH as over-the-top spectacular. We see shepherds who've crept down from dark hills and wise men who journeyed from afar; angels descend in showy splendor, while overhead a star spotlights the baby divine. Surely Bethlehem was a beacon that night, drawing all Israel. Surely no one missed this spectacle. But in fact virtually everyone missed it. God brought forth his Messiah to praise from shepherds and angels, but the world kept right on sleeping.

God had revealed many things about what the Messiah would be like, what he would do, and what would happen to him. He even revealed where he would come from (Micah 5:2). And yet when Messiah finally came, even the devout missed him. The rabbis, who memorized the Scriptures, weren't present to watch Scripture's fulfillment. No huddled masses of the faithful gathered to behold their King. When Jesus's family slipped him out of town to evade Herod's murderous intentions, the path was free of obstruction. Spiritual lethargy and Scriptural ignorance allowed these events to remain almost entirely hidden, but the unexpectedness of the expected Messiah remained a theme throughout Jesus's life.

THE CONCEPTION OF JESUS

Speaking of the unexpected, put yourself in Mary's shoes. When God promised in Genesis 3:15 to send the Messiah

THE FULFILLMENT

through the seed of woman, no one—least of all Mary—could have imagined that the woman would be a young virgin from the middle of nowhere. And yet this was God's choice. He chose Mary and sent the angel Gabriel to tell her so.

> You will conceive and give birth to a son,
> and you will call His name Jesus.
> He will be great
> and will be called the Son of the Most High,
> and the Lord God will give Him
> the throne of His father David.
> He will reign over the house of Jacob forever,
> and His kingdom will have no end.
>
> LUKE 1:31-33

Every pregnancy brings anxiety, but for Mary there was a raft of uncommon concerns. What would it be like, that moment she became pregnant? Gabriel explained that "the Holy Spirit will come upon you, and the power of the Most High will overshadow you" (Luke 1:35). Pious and trusting as Mary was, this news had to fill her with awe and perhaps downright fear. And what about perceptions? The people of Nazareth would have assumed she'd committed adultery, an act sometimes punished by death. And what of her fiancé, Joseph? He would assume the same thing. Mary's miraculous pregnancy, therefore, needed confirmation.

God provided proof first of all to Mary, lest she fear for her sanity. She went to visit her cousin Elizabeth (Luke 1:39-45). Elizabeth herself was miraculously pregnant (her barrenness cured); her baby would become known as John the Baptist. Elizabeth hailed Mary as the mother of the Lord when they greeted one another, a sign to Mary that God had shared news of her state with Elizabeth. When Mary returned from visiting Elizabeth, she was at least three months pregnant and beginning to show. This would have scandalized Joseph, and so God headed off Joseph's reaction by sending an angel to him as well.

Joseph, son of David, don't be afraid to take Mary as your wife, because what has been conceived in her is by the Holy Spirit. She will give birth to a son, and you are to name Him Jesus, because He will save His people from their sins.

MATTHEW 1:20-21

The Birth of Jesus

During the pregnancy, Mary and Joseph must have wondered what this baby—God made flesh—would be like. Will he have a visible aurora? Will his voice boom like thunder? Will he dirty his diapers? When the time finally came, what did they see? A perfectly normal-looking baby. In fact, they might have been tempted to question the angelic messengers. But just then they again received confirmation in the form of shepherds who'd been told by an angel where to find the Messiah (Luke 2:8-20). And eight days later, when Jesus was presented at the temple, the Holy Spirit told the news to Simeon and Anna (Luke 2:25-38).

THE FULFILLMENT

Even so, the news went almost completely unnoticed. In fact when the wise men stopped at Jerusalem to inquire about the Messiah, King Herod was shocked and alarmed (Matthew 2:1-6). He assumed that this prophesied King of kings would want to overthrow his throne, and so he plotted to murder Jesus. At that point it had been more than a year since Jesus had been born (contrary to popular conception, the wise men probably arrived to find a toddler, not an infant). And so Herod cast his deadly net wide by ordering the murder of all male children in Bethlehem who were under two years old. Jesus escaped the plot, but Herod's plan to spoil the prophecy was itself prophesied in Jeremiah 31:15 and supplied further proof that Jesus was the fulfillment of the messianic promise.

As for the wise men, they were important for several reasons. First, they were Gentiles, not Jews. This was a sign that the Messiah is for all peoples, not just Jews. Second, their arrival, prompted by a miraculous sign, was further confirmation that Jesus was the promised Messiah. Third, by bringing gifts to honor Jesus, the wise men gave the family resources that helped meet their financial needs while they were on the run for several years.

FLIGHT AND EARLY LIFE

Before Herod's soldiers carried out their horrible orders, God warned Joseph to escape to Egypt (Matthew 2:13-15). And so it was that the birth of the Savior cost the lives of innocent boys in Bethlehem, yet another evidence of human depravity. The holy family remained in Egypt, living anonymously, until Herod died. Joseph aimed to settle in Bethlehem, but

God sent him back to Nazareth, Mary's tiny hometown. By bringing Jesus from Egypt, God reenacted the exodus of the Jews, the event that freed his people from slavery and made them a people for himself.

Many have speculated about Jesus's childhood. They speculate because the Bible itself is silent about this period. Storytellers love to fill a void, and so by a hundred years or so after Jesus's resurrection, legends of power and wonderment had cropped up about his doings as a child. There's a tale of him making live birds from clay. More controversially, one story depicts him losing his temper and killing a playmate with a word, only to revive him later. These stories are pabulum, tabloid fare that can't be trusted.

The truth is, from the time Jesus returned from Egypt until he was about 30, we know nothing—except one thing. When Jesus was 12 he traveled with his family to Jerusalem for Passover (Luke 2:41-50). After the feast was over, all the families packed up and left town, traveling by caravan. In the great pack and bustle of people, Mary and Joseph didn't realize that Jesus wasn't present. He was nearing manhood and would have been trusted to do what was expected. But Jesus was the expected Messiah, who always did the *un*expected. What he'd done was stay back in Jerusalem, holding court at the temple.

When his parents tracked him down after three days, Jesus was puzzled. "'Why were you searching for Me?' He asked them. 'Didn't you know that I had to be in My Father's house?'" (Luke 2:49). The Bible doesn't say when Jesus began to understand that he is God incarnate. Probably he became more self-aware as he grew out of early childhood.

THE FULFILLMENT

Whenever it was that awareness of divinity dawned on him, it had obviously happened by the time he awed the teachers in the temple. And yet it would be another 18 years before he initiated his public ministry at a wedding in Cana.

FIRST MIRACLE

Jesus had already been teaching some and had called his disciples when he performed his famous banquet sign. When the wine jars gave out, Jesus's mother asked him to do something about it, to save the bride and groom from shame. Had she seen him perform miracles before, privately? Perhaps so. At the very least she was certain he could do it. Jesus responded by converting water to wine in six stone jars, his first miracle recounted in Scripture.

This was more than an attempt to salvage reputations or bless newlyweds. The miracle served to bolster the faith and confidence of Jesus's disciples. Further, the jars of water were used for the rite of purification. Jesus transformed the symbol of purification into something new. The wine is a foreshadowing of his blood (symbolized by wine at the Last Supper), which must be shed in order for us to be purified. Count this as the most unexpected of the expected Messiah's unexpected acts: he came to shed his blood for us.

A SURE THING, SURELY MISSED

The surprising ways in which Jesus fulfilled the messianic prophecies meant that it was certain he is the Messiah, but it also explains why the fulfillments were often overlooked or resisted. Simply put, the Jews expected something else. They wanted a conquering warrior, a king to sweep away Roman occupation and establish Jerusalem as the world's central power. But this wasn't God's purpose for Messiah. He had spiritual aims rather than political ones. He sought permanent solutions, not temporary fixes.

Jesus's teachings threw them off as well. He asserted his divinity (John 8:58), valued women and foreigners (Luke 7:36-50; 10:25-37), resisted the religious establishment (Matthew 23:1-12), and taught forgiveness rather than vengeance (Matthew 5:39). You may think it would've been amazing to see Jesus yourself—a spiritually moving experience—but where would you have stood, actually? Would you have been among those listening in faith, or would you have stood with the crowds that condemned him? Many disbelieved. They had other agendas, priorities Jesus didn't support. They never imagined that the Messiah would be God himself, that he would be born to a peasant girl, grow up anonymously in a backwater town, and allow himself to be killed. Even with Isaiah's prophecies of a suffering servant (Isaiah 53), who could have pictured such a thing? And so it was that many refused Jesus and sought another savior, the age-old mistake repeated again.

REFLECT & DISCUSS

1. Describe a time when you missed out on what God was doing in your life or the lives of those around you.

2. What difference does it make for us that Jesus was born of a virgin?

3. The wise men were foreign Gentile stargazers (likely astrologers) and not Jewish religious leaders. What kind

of signal does that send to non-Jewish people looking for salvation?

4. Jesus performed many miracles, including turning water into wine. What insight does this particular miracle give you about Jesus?

5. Jesus came to be a spiritual savior rather than the political savior most of Israel wanted. Judging by your prayers, what kind of savior are you most often looking for?

CHAPTER 4

THE LIFE

IMAGINE SOMEONE HANDS YOU a single puzzle piece and asks, "What does the whole puzzle look like?" You could take a stab at the answer, but nothing more. Ten people viewing the same piece would give ten different answers.

Taken individually, the Old Testament prophecies about the Messiah are similar to this. The puzzle pieces were handed out piece by piece over the course of thousands of years; each prophecy offered just a glimpse of the whole. You could turn each one every which way, study its details, and still have an incomplete picture of the Messiah.

But the pieces kept coming.

One at a time.

Given by God and recorded in Scripture.

Once all the pieces came together and were seen as a whole, the picture they formed was unmistakably that of Jesus of Nazareth, at least to those who looked with open hearts.

THE PERSON AND WORK OF JESUS

If all the great men of the Old Testament couldn't reverse Adam's curse, what would it take for Jesus to succeed? Nothing less than perfection in his person (who he is) and his work (what he does).

As God in the flesh, Jesus shares in all the attributes of divinity. It doesn't get any more perfect than that. And yet Jesus's divinity wasn't sufficient to make him our Savior.

The way he lived his life—*as a genuine human*—was just as vital. Had Jesus merely descended from heaven and been ushered straight to the cross, he couldn't have served as Messiah. He would have lacked a genuine human nature, or he would have been a human who lived no genuine human life. In order to represent us before God, Jesus had to be fully God, fully human, and live a fully human life flawlessly. He had to be one of us—a *holy* one of us—to mediate between unholy humanity and holy God.

When Adam fell into sin, he dragged us all down with him. By inescapable inheritance, we are born with a sin nature and are unable to please God (Psalm 51:5; Romans 3:23). This applies to every human, except Jesus. Because he was conceived through the Holy Spirit, Jesus didn't inherit Adam's sin. He was born pure, wholly without enslavement to sin. This doesn't mean he couldn't have sinned or couldn't be tempted. Hebrews 4:15 makes this clear:

> For we do not have a high priest who is unable to sympathize with our weaknesses, but One who has been tested in every way as we are, yet without sin.

Jesus can identify with the things we face—the lies, the enticements, the shortcuts, the temptations designed to destroy us. He resisted sin at all points not because he was detached from temptation (he wasn't), but because he deliberately obeyed the entire law of God. Nowhere is this clearer than when he was tempted by Satan at the start of his ministry (Matthew 4). After undergoing baptism to identify himself with his people and signify the purification he would provide for them, Jesus spent 40 days fasting in the wilderness. Imagine what a man is reduced to after 40 days of hunger and solitude. It's in this condition that Jesus faced Satan, the tempter who offered to meet all of his needs. Satan may have a gift of ingenuity, but he doesn't show it in tactical variety. His temptations with Jesus are the same ones he used on Adam and Eve. He tempted Jesus to believe that . . .

- God doesn't meet all our needs (Matthew 4:3).
- God's Word must be tested before trusted (Matthew 4:6).
- God was holding back his best (Matthew 4:8-9).

Jesus's tactic each time was to respond by quoting Scripture, to squelch lies with truth. Temptations have no power when you see behind them using the lens of Scripture. Behind it all—stones turned to bread, divine interventions to prevent a fatal fall, promises of worldly power—Jesus knew there was only Satan's hunger for destruction. And so Jesus denied every temptation. For this reason, he "is able to help those who are tested" (Hebrews 2:18).

The prophet Isaiah foretold that Messiah would be . . .

. . . despised and rejected by men,
a man of suffering who knew what sickness was.
He was like someone people turned away from;

THE LIFE

He was despised, and we didn't value Him.
Yet He Himself bore our sicknesses,
and He carried our pains.

ISAIAH 53:3-4

By "sickness" Isaiah meant sin. And notice that the sickness Messiah bore wasn't his own, but *ours*. Peter recognizes Jesus as the fulfillment of Isaiah's prophecy and says, "He did not commit sin, and no deceit was found in His mouth" (1 Peter 2:22). John says something similar: "He was revealed so that He might take away sins, and there is no sin in Him" (1 John 3:5).

JESUS RELIVES AND PERFECTS ISRAEL'S HISTORY

In many ways Jesus's biography is a retelling of Israel's history. By God's design, Jesus retraced and perfected some of the key events through which the nation had lived. Examples include:

- The Hebrews left Egypt for the promised land in their early history; Jesus did the same thing (Exodus 12–14; Matthew 2:13-20). God used the first exodus to make a national people for himself (Israel), and the second to make a transnational people for himself (the Church).
- God gave the law to Moses at Mount Sinai; Jesus restated the law in his Sermon on the Mount (Exodus 20; Matthew 5-7).
- Jesus said, "Just as Moses lifted up the snake in the wilderness [see Numbers 21:4-9], so the Son of Man must

be lifted up, so that everyone who believes in Him will have eternal life" (John 3:14-15).

Jesus is a symbolic do-over for the nation of Israel, but he got right all the things they got wrong. He also proved to be the reality behind the symbols found in Israel's national life. For example, in the sacrificial system a high priest mediated on behalf of the people, and a sacrificial animal symbolically took on the sins of the people and was slain to appease God's wrath (Leviticus 16). Jesus is our high priest, and he was slain on our behalf because he became sin for us (Hebrews 4:14-16; 2 Corinthians 5:21).

JESUS AS PROPHET, PRIEST, AND KING

God used prophets, priests, and kings to reveal himself and rule over his people. *Good, bad,* and *indifferent* would be fair terms for summing up the quality of men filling these roles. Each one occupied the office temporarily and imperfectly and thus helped point to the One who would someday fulfill all three roles perfectly and forever: the Messiah.

Through prophets God revealed his will and his plans. Prophets weren't inspired fortunetellers or prediction makers; they were God's mouthpieces. They spoke and wrote with God's authority, which means that to disbelieve a prophet was to disbelieve God. Jesus spoke with the authority of God, but not in the same way as the prophets. The difference is that Jesus spoke not just *from* God but *as* God. His authority wasn't a derivative quality. God the Son spoke as the final prophet. He gave us the last word, and he himself is the Word (John 1).

God appointed priests to represent the people before him so the people could be in a right relationship with him. The priests wore special vestments and lived by special rules to set them apart as holy, dedicated to sacred purposes such as offering sacrifices on behalf of the people. Their work was never finally effective, however, as the sacrifices and rites had to be repeated over and over (Hebrews 10:1-4). Jesus came as the final priest, the High Priest to end ritual and sacrifice by offering himself as the finality of both. He now sits at the right hand of the Father because the work of paying for sins is complete.

Kingship was a concession to the people's desire to have a human king, just like the nations around them. Kings were meant to be benevolent representatives of God, shepherds of the nation who kept God's laws. All fell short of this, many of them woefully so. With each regal failure, God taught the Hebrews lessons on the unreliability of human leaders. If ever they were to have a perfect king, that king would have to be the Promised One, the Messiah. Jesus is King over all creation because he is both Creator and the One for whom it was all created (Colossians 1:16). All thrones before and after point to his as the Throne of thrones.

MISSING THE OBVIOUS

If so many details about the Messiah were foretold in the Old Testament, and if Jesus fulfilled all the prophecies and symbols, why did so many people overlook or even reject him? Part of the problem is that at the time of Jesus, the Jews were ruled by Rome and wanted to break free. Although they knew a messiah had been promised to them, they thought what they needed most was political liberation. They were thinking in terms of a national savior, not a Savior of nations. They were distracted from God's Messiah by looking for a messiah of their own making.

Another factor leading many to reject Jesus has to do with the *who* and the *how* of his ministry. Rather than courting favor among the powerful, Jesus spent most of his time among outcasts and hoi polloi, the common people who wielded no influence in Jerusalem, much less Rome. When Jesus did engage powerful people, he opposed them for their abuses and spiritual pride.

But by far the most significant factor explaining why many rejected Jesus is that they were suffering from the very problem he came to solve: spiritual deadness. There's a price to accepting Jesus as Messiah, and most weren't willing to pay it then or now.

None of this is a misfit with what Scripture foretold about the Messiah. Isaiah said it all many hundreds of years before Jesus was born: "He was despised and rejected by men" (Isaiah 53:3). The Messiah was intended to conquer his enemies not by military strength or political ascendancy, but through rejection, humiliation, and substitutionary death.

REFLECT & DISCUSS

1. Jesus sympathizes with our weakness. In what area of life do you need God's sympathy right now?

2. When Satan tempted Jesus to sin, the Lord answered each temptation by quoting Scripture. What topics of Scripture do you need to access in order to turn away Satan's temptations?

3. Jesus perfected Old Testament history by fulfilling the law, which the Israelites consistently failed to do. How does this bring hope for you?

4. As the ultimate prophet, Jesus speaks the perfect truth. Make a list of issues in your life where you need to be reminded of God's truth so you can turn away the world's errors.

5. Jesus has all of the power as the King of kings. What areas of your life have you been withholding from him that you should now surrender?

CHAPTER 5

THE TEACHINGS

THERE ARE MANY WOULD-BE TEACHERS in the world, people burning to spread a message. Gifted with words and vision and oftentimes catapulted by outsized personality, they seek to lead change or protect tradition. Or maybe they just want to make a name for themselves. The question we must ask every time is: Should we listen? Not every teaching ought to be believed, and some visions are best left unfulfilled.

Jesus isn't the only religious leader vying for our attention. Countless others have come and gone, claiming to have a word from divinity. Why should we think Jesus is any different? One reason is his fulfillment of prophecies. He couldn't contrive his place of birth or his miraculous conception, how others received or rejected him, or the events in his betrayal and crucifixion. That Jesus fulfilled the prophecies shows that he's the one sent by God and that God orchestrated countless variables so that Jesus's life lined up with all that had been foretold about the Messiah.

Another factor separating Jesus is his life's work. Others had come renouncing wealth and fame, but none were sinless (1 John 3:5), turned water to wine (John 2:1-11), or raised the dead (Mark 5:21-43; John 11). Others came and showed care for outcasts, but none walked on water (Matthew 14:22-33), healed the blind (John 9), or demonstrated omniscience (John 16:30).

THE TEACHINGS

The fulfilled prophecies and divine works show that Jesus isn't just another teacher; he's *the* teacher. Unbelievers commonly describe him as a great moral teacher but insist he was nothing more. There are two problems with this: Jesus's moral teachings aren't unique, and some of his other teachings are abhorrent if he's not God.

First, the moral teachings. Jesus really didn't break much new ground there. Ideas such as the equality of all people and the Golden Rule (treat others the way you want to be treated) didn't originate with Jesus.

Second, Jesus's teachings weren't limited to morality. Much of what he said—and what makes him unique—emphasized his identity as God the Son. He didn't merely teach *about* morality; he claimed to be the *source* of morality.

DID JESUS TEACH THAT HE IS GOD?

Scripture never records Jesus saying, "I am God," but it hardly matters. It was the Roman era, after all, a time when pagan gods proliferated. The emperor could be hailed as a god, and the Egyptians had practiced a similar imperial cult. In that context, to go around saying, "I'm God," would just lump you in with other men of renown. Jesus was far too savvy to fall in line with that.

FORGIVENESS OF SINS

One way Jesus claimed to be God was through granting forgiveness of sins. That's more subtle than saying, "I am God," but it's no less clear. After all, who can forgive sin but God? Bystanders understood this. You can tell by the way they reacted. Take, for instance, the story of the paralytic who was lowered through a roof.

Seeing their faith, Jesus told the paralytic,
"Son, your sins are forgiven."
But some of the scribes were sitting there,
thinking to themselves: "Why does He speak like
this? He's blaspheming! Who can forgive sins
but God alone?"
Right away Jesus understood in His spirit that
they were thinking like this within themselves and
said to them, "Why are you thinking these things
in your hearts? Which is easier: to say to the
paralytic, 'Your sins are forgiven,' or to say, 'Get
up, pick up your mat, and walk'? But so you may
know that the Son of Man has authority on earth
to forgive sins," He told the paralytic, "I tell you:
get up, pick up your mat, and go home."
Immediately he got up, picked up the mat, and
went out in front of everyone. As a result, they
were all astounded and gave glory to God, saying,
"We have never seen anything like this!"

MARK 2:5-12

The scribes were riled at Jesus's claim to forgive sins, but Jesus neutralized them by performing a visible work (the miracle) that verified his right to do the invisible work (forgive sins). By this ingenious move, Jesus claimed to be God, but did so without being so tactless as to blurt out "I'm God" and incur immediate opposition that might shortcut his mission.

AUTHORITY TO TEACH

If you want to teach nuclear physics, you can't just strike out on your own and do so. You have to invest years of study at sanctioned institutions and earn the degrees. Doing this, you become a bona fide nuclear physicist.

If you can't teach physics without first earning the authority to do so, how much more so when the subject is God? That's why the scribes and Pharisees were trained not to teach anything new. Their aim was to preserve and explain Scripture and the traditions they had inherited. The problem is they ended up adding human rules in an attempt to ward off corruption. They poisoned the very well they meant to keep pure.

One of the things that made Jesus a threat to the Pharisees is that he taught on his own authority rather than appealing to tradition. For example, in Matthew 5:21-22 Jesus says:

> "You have heard that it was said to our ancestors, Do not murder, and whoever murders will be subject to judgment. But I tell you, everyone who is angry with his brother will be subject to judgment."

Matthew 7:28-29 says that after the Sermon on the Mount, "the crowds were astonished at His teaching, because He was teaching them like one who had authority, and not like their scribes." By teaching on his own authority, Jesus claimed to be God. It was plain to see, and it explains why people reacted so strongly to him, whether for or against.

JESUS, THE I AM

Jesus also claimed to be God by using for himself names belonging to God. For example, in John 8:58-59, he says:

"I assure you: Before Abraham was, I am."
At that, they picked up stones to throw at Him.

They didn't pick up stones because he'd used bad grammar. They knew what he meant, knew he was claiming to be God. Jesus had picked up language from a seminal Old Testament text, where God had used the name "I AM" for himself when speaking to Moses from the burning bush (Exodus 3:14).

WORSHIP IS FOR GOD ALONE

You've heard that Jesus once walked on water. Just as significant is what went down afterward. Once Jesus got into the boat, "Those in the boat worshiped Him and said, 'Truly You are the Son of God!'" (Matthew 14:33). Now if Jesus were a great moral teacher but merely a man, here was his chance to correct a grievously wrong perception. He'd have *raced* to deny his divinity here if he needed to. But he didn't need to. He didn't need to because he is, as the disciples concluded, God the Son.

THE TEACHINGS

SOURCE OF LIFE AND SALVATION

The Pharisees, Sadducees, and scribes constantly argued with Jesus. They came to hate and fear him so much that they plotted to kill him. The core of their disagreement was over how to attain righteousness. The religious leaders placed their hope in, well, *religion*. They thought that by keeping the rules (many of which they'd invented), they could earn salvation. Jesus exposed this as a lie. He showed that no one could keep God's law perfectly, and that he did for us what we couldn't do for ourselves.

Jesus always found arresting ways to stake such claims. For example, here's how he pointed out that we can't make ourselves spiritually alive: "I assure you: Unless you eat the flesh of the Son of Man and drink His blood, you do not have life in yourselves" (John 6:53). Elsewhere he said: "I am the way, the truth, and the life. No one comes to the Father except through Me" (John 14:6). Anyone claiming Jesus shied away from divinity claims needs to actually read the Gospels.

THE KINGDOM OF GOD

We think of salvation as escape from hell. It's an understandable fixation! Jesus himself stoked the fire with all his talk about a fiery furnace (Mark 9:42-49), outer darkness (Matthew 8:12), and torment (Luke 16:23). But he also had a lot to say about what we're saved *to*—the kingdom of God. From Genesis to Revelation, God's plan is to make a people for himself; he pulls from every nation and every ethnicity to do it, and he grants citizenship by grace.

AFTER CHRISTMAS

Our citizenship comes with life-giving obligations and opportunities. We're to be replicators, drawing people into the kingdom. Jesus transforms us for this task. In the Sermon on the Mount (Matthew 5–7), he tells us to embrace humility so that we may be exalted; he bids us show mercy so that we may find mercy; we're told to guard the heart, the seat of all evil; he says we're blessed when persecuted for his sake, so never be ashamed of his name; he teaches us how to pray, how to forgive, what to think of material possessions; he talks about holy persistence, the dangers of judging, and the joy of giving. Yes, Jesus is holy God and will stand as Judge of all in the end, but he also came to lead us into abundant life.

The Love of God

Does God really love this world? He cursed it and marked it for judgment nearly at its inception. He sentenced our misbehaving first parents to death, exiled them, and possibly never spoke to them again. The years of silence stretched out for centuries as humanity ran headlong into debauchery and violence. Fed up, God killed all life on earth save eight humans and the animals that filed into Noah's boat. Later revelations described our sinful unworthiness (Isaiah 64:6), our inability to fix it (Ephesians 2:1), and a fiery eternal pit (2 Thessalonians 1:4-12) with a broad onramp (Matthew 7:13).

Does God really love this world?

God does love this world, and Jesus is the best proof. He showed God's love by the fact that he came as one of us. He entered the enemy camp not to overthrow us, but to win us over. Most amazing of all, his winning us over involved submitting himself to history's greatest travesty.

THE TEACHINGS

REFLECT & DISCUSS

1. What teaching from the Bible do you find most difficult to obey? Why?

2. Jesus used the name of God from the Old Testament—I AM—to describe himself. Why do you think the religious leaders rejected this claim rather than accept it and follow Jesus?

3. In Jesus's ministry, he pointed out the difference between seeking religion and seeking righteousness. How would you describe the difference? What tempts you to seek out the wrong one?

4. Becoming a Christian is more than just getting out of an eternity in hell. Describe some positive outcomes in your life from when you became a member of God's kingdom.

5. The Bible states, "God is love" (1 John 4:8). How would you describe the love of God to a friend who is not a Christian?

CHAPTER 6

THE CROSS

YOU BEAR THE MARK OF DEATH. God placed it on you because of his curse against sin. But death isn't your purpose, and the time and manner of your death are unknown to you.

Not so for Jesus. Death was his purpose in life, and he knew the *how* and the *why*, the *when* and the *where*, from a long way off. In fact these things were determined for him from all eternity. The ageless plan, crafted by the Father and agreed upon by the Son, came together perfectly when Jesus was mocked, beaten, and executed during Israel's high holiday, the Passover.

Jesus knew, Jesus planned, Jesus walked forward into voluntary death, but this was no suicide. It was self-sacrifice on behalf of the human race, a mission foretold in the prophecies (e.g., Psalm 22; Isaiah 52:13–53:12).

A TRIUMPHAL ENTRANCE

Jerusalem was packed with pilgrims when Jesus arrived. Fame and controversy preceded him, but questions about his identity persisted. His revelations had been given mostly in the countryside, not among the power elite in the Holy City. Now was Jesus's chance to make his identity clear on Israel's biggest stage, and he seized it by . . . *riding into town on a donkey?*

THE CROSS

Rejoice greatly, Daughter Zion!
Shout in triumph, Daughter Jerusalem!
Look, your King is coming to you;
He is righteous and victorious,
humble and riding on a donkey,
on a colt, the foal of a donkey.

ZECHARIAH 9:9

Thus Jesus fulfilled another prophecy, but skeptics complain that anyone claiming to be messiah could ride a donkey into town and thus contrive the fulfillment. That's true, but a pretender would've been hard pressed to elicit such high praise from the crowds (Matthew 21:8-11), and a pretender couldn't possibly have fulfilled all the other prophecies that were outside human control, including Messiah's looming death at the hands of others.

A Foretold Death

As Jesus entered Jerusalem, he knew that his hour of death was near (John 12:23). He didn't keep this from his disciples. He had foretold them many aspects of his suffering and execution. Among the details, he said he would be . . .

- betrayed (Matthew 26:21; Mark 9:31; 14:18; Luke 22:21; John 13:18)
- made to suffer many things from the elders, chief priests, and scribes (Matthew 16:21; Mark 8:31; 9:31; 10:33)

- given to the Gentiles, who would mock him, spit on him, and flog him (Mark 10:33-34; Luke 18:32)
- killed (Matthew 16:21; Mark 8:31; 9:31; 10:34; Luke 18:33)
- raised the third day (Matthew 16:21; Mark 8:31; 9:31; 10:34; Luke 18:33)

No false messiah could know all of these things or arrange for their contrivance. Most obviously, a mere man can't control the manner of his death when that death is at the hands of others, much less arrange for his own resurrection.

ESCALATION AND BETRAYAL

If the religious leaders still entertained doubts about Jesus's potential to dislodge their grip on the people, those doubts were banished as he entered town. The praises, shouts of Hosanna, the sign of the donkey, the palm fronds laid down for the reception of royalty—these all proved that Jesus needed to be neutralized, and *fast*. But how to do that with the crowds following him? Already the people's champion, he was quickly becoming their Messiah. Nab Jesus in plain sight and the whole city might boil over. What the leaders needed was a turncoat, someone who could arrange a clandestine capture. That's exactly what they found in Jesus's treasurer, Judas Iscariot.

Scripture never says what drove Judas to betrayal. We know that he was a thief (John 12:6) and that he sought payment for turning traitor (Matthew 26:15-16). Guilt stricken, he returned the money before killing himself. In any case, Jesus wasn't surprised by any of it. At the Last Supper he exposed Judas as the one who would betray him (John 13:26). Judas immediately left, probably intent on bringing the authorities down on Jesus right away. If so, Jesus made him work a little harder for his pay, for he led the disciples back to Gethsemane for the night.

We're getting down to the really hard things now. Jesus knew it, and he prayed to be spared. The inquisitions, lashings, mockery, and crucifixion—he foreknew each detail. He sweated blood (or "like drops of blood") thinking about it all, especially the fact that he would become sin on the cross and be separated from the Father as he bore divine wrath against sin (Luke 22:44; 2 Corinthians 5:21; Mark 15:34).

Judas tramped into the garden with soldiers in tow. Some of the disciples wanted to fight, but that wasn't Jesus's purpose. He accepted Judas's kiss, accepted all that he prayed to be spared from because his mission was everything. "Am I not to drink the cup the Father has given Me?" (John 18:11). It wasn't a question.

JUSTICE MISCARRIED

Jesus endured six trials, three religious and three civil. He never stood a chance. One trial was before Annas, the influential former high priest. Another was before a partial gathering of the Sanhedrin (Pharisees and Sadducees who governed religious life). The third was before the whole Sanhedrin. The first two were held before dawn and were chaotic. They probably expected Judas to be a witness, but he skipped out, likely wracked with guilt in some dark corner. In the end, they didn't need witnesses because Jesus implicated himself. When asked whether he was the Messiah, Son of God, he said *yes* (Matthew 26:63-64). To the unbelieving Sanhedrin, this was blasphemy and warrant for execution. But the Jews lacked the power of execution. The Romans kept that for themselves as a means of control. If the Sanhedrin wanted Jesus dead, they'd need to convince Pontius Pilate, Roman governor of Judea.

The Jewish leaders resented Roman rule, but watch them now morph into Caesar's watchdogs. They warned Pilate that Jesus was subverting Caesar by calling himself a king and by dodging taxes (Luke 23:2). Pilate saw through this nonsense and perceived Jesus's innocence, but passed him on to Herod. Herod just wanted a magic show, but Jesus refused to work miracles or be grilled with questions. Stumped, Herod and his men mocked Jesus and sent him *back* to Pilate, absurdly draped in a royal robe (Luke 23:8-12).

Pilate was in a fix now. No way he wanted Jesus killed, but neither did he want a riot on his hands, for the Jewish leadership had incited a mob to oppose Jesus. Seeking a middle way, Pilate said he'd have Jesus scourged, a brutal punishment. A whip with bits of glass and metal woven into the ends was used to rip away flesh and bore down to the bone. The scourging would reduce Jesus to a tattered, bloody mess, but the mob wanted more. "Crucify! Crucify Him!" (Luke 23:21).

Exasperated, Pilate washed his hands in front of them all. He had Jesus scourged and turned him over for final injustice.

CURSED IS HE WHO HANGS ON A TREE

Crucifixion was so barbaric that Roman law forbade Romans from being subjected to it. Victims were made to carry their crossbar to the execution site, where they were nailed to the beams at the wrists and ankles. The legs were kept bent at the knees, which, once the cross was positioned upright, made breathing difficult because the victim's body weight would tug hard at the nailed wrists. The eventual results were dislocated shoulders and collapsed lungs. To breathe, victims had to get the weight off their lungs, but they couldn't pull up by their ruined wrists and dislocated shoulders, and so they had to push up on the nails embedded in their ankles. This cycle of pushing and resting, pushing and resting, continued until asphyxiation, blood loss, shock, or a combination of these killed them. Victims in good shape could last a week; those who'd been scourged first died much sooner.

Jesus spoke several times from the cross. He granted salvation to one of the criminals crucified beside him (Luke 23:43), committed his mother to John's care (John 19:27), and cried out, "My God, My God, why have You forsaken me?" as he paid for our sins (Matthew 27:46). Finally, he called out, "Father, into Your hands I entrust My spirit" (Luke 23:46) and "It is finished!" (John 19:30).

At the moment of his death, the veil that set off the most holy part of the temple was torn from top to bottom (Matthew 27:51). This act of God indicated that the ceremonial laws had been fulfilled by Jesus's atoning sacrifice. The temple and its priests were no longer necessary. An earthquake also struck, and many dead saints were raised (Matthew 27:52). The darkness that had fallen on the land around noon started to clear.

AN UNEXPECTED DEATH

Jesus's death shocked his disciples. He had told them it was coming, but they found it insensible, *impossible*. Messiah was supposed to unseat Roman rule and elevate the disciples to power (Mark 10:35-45)! Raise the dead but subject *himself* to death? Nonsense. They couldn't comprehend it or stand to watch the crucifixion. Nailed to a cross in the midst of a crowd, Jesus died essentially alone.

Crucifixion victims were often left hanging long after they died. Sun baked, bloated, rotted, their bodies served as a warning to respect Roman authority. What parts weren't eaten or carried off by carrion birds were eventually thrown into common graves or trash heaps, but something unusual was done with Jesus's body. Perhaps due to Pilate's awareness that he'd been unjustly executed, Jesus's body was given to Joseph of Arimathea for burial.

It was late by now. Sabbath was coming, the day of strict rest. Jesus's female disciples from Galilee hastily prepared his body for burial lest they be caught working when Sabbath began at nightfall (Luke 23:54-56). Joseph wrapped the body in a cloth and placed it in his tomb. The women watched, noting the location. They would return with perfumes and spices after the Sabbath and do a better job of honoring Jesus, their Lord of life who had succumbed to death.

REFLECT & DISCUSS

1. How often do you think about death and what comes next?

2. Judas betrayed Jesus for money. Think through your spiritual journey and list some of the trivial things for which you've betrayed faithfulness to Jesus.

3. The Bible states that Jesus became sin for us on the cross. How does the extent of his work on your behalf change the way you view daily temptations?

4. Herod washed his hands symbolically to say he wanted nothing to do with sentencing Jesus. In what ways are you evading responsibility for justice and spiritual truth in your life?

5. The act of crucifixion was barbaric, and yet Jesus's greatest pain was endurance of the Father's judgment. Imagine the sum total of all sins in history, and imagine God's wrath against them poured onto Jesus in a moment of judgment. Discuss your response to Jesus's sacrifice on your behalf.

CHAPTER 7

THE RESURRECTION

JESUS TAUGHT MANY THINGS that couldn't be fact-checked by his listeners. That's the nature of making claims about unseen realities like salvation. Jesus understood this. That's one reason he performed miracles. Healings and resurrections gave powerful evidence that Jesus was truly the divine Son. But now he was dead and gone. What could it mean? Was he not the Messiah after all?

The disciples must have wondered. We see no evidence in Scripture that any of them felt hopeful in the aftermath of Jesus's death and burial. That they were hopeless despite Jesus's resurrection prophecy (Matthew 16:21) indicates the depth of their misunderstanding about Messiah's two-part mission (first to die, then to rise).

While forgetful disciples mourned, unbelieving Pharisees recalled Jesus's prophecy perfectly well. Not with faith or hope, but with cynical dread. They feared that Jesus's followers would steal the body and fake a resurrection fulfillment, and so they asked Pilate for help. Pilate granted soldiers to stand guard at the tomb. A crowd was now gathered around the tomb 24/7. Subsequent events, whatever direction they took, would have no shortage of witnesses.

THE RESURRECTION

RESURRECTION PROOF (MATTHEW 28; MARK 16; LUKE 24; JOHN 20-21; ACTS 1)

What lifted Jesus's followers out of fear and despondency? The Bible is clear: angels descended and opened the tomb Sunday morning in view of the soldiers and the women who'd come to tend to the body. That opened tomb proved to be an *empty* tomb, and that resulted in bribes (the soldiers were bribed by the religious leaders to say the disciples stole the body), suspicion (Mary Magdalene first assumed someone had indeed stolen the body), and belief (John, when he saw the empty tomb and empty grave cloth). And then the appearances began. First to Mary as she lingered at the tomb; after her, many more as Jesus met his followers on roadways, behind locked doors, by a lakeside in Galilee, and unnamed places over the next 40 days. At one point he even appeared to around 500 people at once. So began Christianity, a faith entirely dependent on the literal resurrection of Jesus from the dead (1 Corinthians 15:1-19).

BUT IS IT TRUE?

New Testament scholars range widely in their beliefs. Some double as preachers; others are avowed atheists. Even so, virtually all agree on a dozen or so key facts surrounding Jesus's crucifixion and aftermath. These are known as the "minimal facts" since they are widely accepted. Scholars who reject Jesus's resurrection have to explain what happened to Jesus in a way that takes stock of these facts. None of the skeptical theories is able to do this. Below we state *in italics* six of the minimal facts and see that the best way to account for them is to accept Jesus's resurrection as literally true.

Jesus was crucified. Jesus's crucifixion was sometimes described as being hung on a tree. That's a reference to the wood of the cross, not an alternate account of his execution. Without question Jesus was executed on a cross.

Jesus died. The one major attempt to deny that Jesus died is known as the swoon theory, and it's never garnered serious support because it hypothesizes that Jesus suffered the scourging, crucifixion, spear through the side, and yet survived and was able to unwrap his burial cloths, remove the two-ton tomb stone from inside the tomb, and present himself as able-bodied, whole, and divine!

Jesus was buried in a tomb. A few scholars try to deny Jesus's tomb burial because crucifixion victims were rarely allowed proper burial. However, the fact that proper burial was rare doesn't mean there weren't exceptions, and the evidence for an exception in Jesus's case is, well, *exceptional.* No alternative theory existed in the ancient literature, and the pervasiveness of the empty tomb theme among believers and unbelievers alike relies on there having been a tomb burial.

Jesus's tomb was found empty three days after his burial. Some skeptics suggest Jesus's followers went to the wrong tomb and thus mistakenly sparked off resurrection belief, but Jewish sources such as the *Toledoth Jesu* record that the disciples stole Jesus's body from his tomb. That means non-Christian Jews acknowledged that Jesus's followers went to the correct tomb. Justin Martyr, a Christian theologian who wrote around AD 150, also says non-Christian Jews alleged that Jesus's followers had stolen his body. Further, the New

THE RESURRECTION

Testament itself says this is what non-Christian Jews taught (Matthew 28:11-15). And so early believers and nonbelievers alike agreed that Jesus was buried and that the tomb—*the correct tomb*—was found empty. Naturally both groups knew the exact tomb Jesus was buried in or else they wouldn't have agreed on the fact that Jesus's tomb was found empty. Nonbelievers thus invented the theft claim in order to deny that the empty tomb indicated a resurrection. The theft claim makes no sense, however, for if nonbelievers stole the body in an attempt to dishearten Jesus's followers, they would've produced the body right away once they realized that their ploy had backfired and created a resurrection rumor. Any idea that *believers* stole Jesus's body in order to create a resurrection hoax fails on several counts, including the problem of them having to get past the guards at the tomb, and the problem of them paying such a high cost for perpetuating a claim they knew to be false. Why stick to your resurrection claims when (1) you know the claims are false and (2) the claims cause you persecution?

Followers of Jesus believed they encountered him after his death. Even scholars who disbelieve Jesus's resurrection acknowledge that his earliest followers were convinced that they had seen him alive again after his death. Attempts to argue that they were mistaken have included allegations of group hallucination (based on religious hype or drug use!) and wishful thinking. It's far-fetched to think a group hallucination could happen even once and lead people to believe in a resurrection, but multiple times, and with hallucinations convincing even committed nonbelievers of Jesus's resurrection? Who is it that's doing the wishful thinking here?

AFTER CHRISTMAS

Enemies of Jesus believed they encountered him after his death. An enemy of Jesus or someone who disbelieved would require very convincing proof before switching sides. One such person was Jesus's half brother, James. During Jesus's ministry, James disbelieved (John 7:5) and thought Jesus was out of his mind (Mark 3:20). Yet after Jesus's resurrection, James became not just a believer, but leader of the Jerusalem church. One who was more like an outright enemy was Saul of Tarsus, who became the apostle Paul. Saul was an educated and committed Pharisee who saw Jesus as a heretic. That's why he persecuted Jesus's followers (Acts 8–9). He was on his way to Tarsus when something happened that changed him forever. As a result of an encounter with the risen Jesus, Paul gave up all comfort and privilege and spent the rest of his life spreading resurrection belief. He was beaten, imprisoned, hungry, shipwrecked, homeless, and according to tradition, beheaded. Did Paul make such a costly life change on the basis of flimsy evidence? If so, wouldn't he have backed out upon further reflection, especially as his new beliefs began to cost him all comfort? The only sensible conclusion is that Paul became a Christian based on what he felt was indisputable evidence.

THE MEANING OF CHRISTMAS

The wood of the manger evokes the wood of the cross, for Jesus came as a babe so that he could eventually serve as our sacrifice. This was necessary because we've broken God's moral laws, which serve as guidelines for defining God's holiness and expectations. Any *un*holy act or disposition is *anti-*God. This means you personally are guilty of aggressions against your Maker. The moral fabric of the universe would tear apart if God let such rebellion go unpunished, for this would mean that his character doesn't matter.

God won't allow such contempt, and so we need atonement. To *atone* is to make right a broken relationship. What does God require for atonement? In the Old Testament he revealed that animal sacrifices should be made. The lifeblood of sinless bulls and goats was spilled onto Hebrew altars in expression of humanity's need for pardon, but this was merely provisional. The blood of animals cannot serve as an adequate replacement for the errant humans to whom God's wrath is due. To serve as an adequate substitute in God's atonement program, the sacrificial victim needs to be sinless, truly representative of humanity, and able to bear on his lone moral frame the debt owed by countless sinners. Obviously this describes a need for human sacrifice. More to the point: a *super*human sacrifice. This is the most breathtaking reality of the Bible. The holy God who made humans in his image required that one of his image bearers, a morally perfect human being, stand in the place of his fellows and give satisfaction for the boundless sin debt.

What man could be adequate for such a task? Only one: Jesus the divine Messiah, sent from heaven to be a human and a stand-in for Adam's stray children. Jesus lived as the ideal human. He loved God above all, obeyed him always, and loved his neighbors as himself. Due to his perfect righteousness and his divine capacities to endure the Father's infinite wrath against sins, Jesus presented himself as the only sufficient substitute for our death penalty. Therefore, on the cross Jesus endured not just the punishment that men handed out but also *God's* punishment against sin as the divine holy nature struck the curse Jesus had become. Jesus *became sin* so that God could judge sin in human flesh and thereby satisfy the requirements of his justice. By faith in Christ's death and resurrection we enjoy pardon from God, not because God let us off the hook, but because Jesus satisfied God's wrath by enduring the blows that were due us. We can live because *he* died and lives again—*for us*.

REFLECT & DISCUSS

1. Why were Jesus's followers so despondent at his death when he had foretold it to them?

2. Why do you think the religious leaders persisted in their unbelief even after Jesus's tomb was found empty and people reported that he was seen alive again?

3. Have you ever doubted the resurrection of Jesus? Describe the difference it makes to you that even doubters came to believe.

4. In your own words, describe the meaning of *atonement*. Also, describe relationships in your life that have been atoned. What part did you play?

5. Take into consideration the true meaning of Christmas. How will that change the way you celebrate Christmas?

LUKE

1 Many have undertaken to compile a narrative about the events that have been fulfilled[A] among us, ²just as the original eyewitnesses and servants of the word handed them down to us. ³It also seemed good to me, since I have carefully investigated everything from the very first, to write to you in an orderly sequence, most honorable Theophilus, ⁴so that you may know the certainty of the things about which you have been instructed.[B]

⁵In the days of King Herod of Judea, there was a priest of Abijah's division[C] named Zechariah. His wife was from the daughters of Aaron, and her name was Elizabeth. ⁶Both were righteous in God's sight, living without blame according to all the commands and requirements of the Lord. ⁷But they had no children[D] because Elizabeth could not conceive,[E] and both of them were well along in years.[F]

⁸When his division was on duty and he was serving as priest before God, ⁹it happened that he was chosen by lot, according to the custom of the priesthood, to enter the sanctuary of the Lord and burn incense. ¹⁰At the hour of incense the whole assembly of the people was praying outside. ¹¹An angel of the Lord appeared to him, standing to the right of the altar of incense. ¹²When Zechariah saw him, he was startled and overcome with fear.[G] ¹³But the angel said to him:

> Do not be afraid, Zechariah,
> because your prayer has been heard.
> Your wife Elizabeth will bear you a son,
> and you will name him John.
> ¹⁴ There will be joy and delight for you,
> and many will rejoice at his birth.
> ¹⁵ For he will be great in the sight
>   of the Lord
> and will never drink wine or beer.
> He will be filled with the Holy Spirit
> while still in his mother's womb.
> ¹⁶ He will turn many of the sons of Israel
> to the Lord their God.
> ¹⁷ And he will go before Him
> in the spirit and power of Elijah,
> to turn the hearts of fathers
> to their children,

> and the disobedient
> to the understanding of the righteous,
> to make ready for the Lord
> a prepared people.

¹⁸"How can I know this?" Zechariah asked the angel. "For I am an old man, and my wife is well along in years."[H]

¹⁹The angel answered him, "I am Gabriel, who stands in the presence of God, and I was sent to speak to you and tell you this good news. ²⁰Now listen! You will become silent and unable to speak until the day these things take place, because you did not believe my words, which will be fulfilled in their proper time."

²¹Meanwhile, the people were waiting for Zechariah, amazed that he stayed so long in the sanctuary. ²²When he did come out, he could not speak to them. Then they realized that he had seen a vision in the sanctuary. He kept making signs to them and remained speechless. ²³When the days of his ministry were completed, he went back home.

²⁴After these days his wife Elizabeth conceived and kept herself in seclusion for five months. She said, ²⁵"The Lord has done this for me. He has looked with favor in these days to take away my disgrace among the people."

²⁶In the sixth month, the angel Gabriel was sent by God to a town in Galilee called Nazareth, ²⁷to a virgin engaged to a man named Joseph, of the house of David. The virgin's name was Mary. ²⁸And the angel came to her and said, "Rejoice, favored woman! The Lord is with you."[I] ²⁹But she was deeply troubled by this statement, wondering what kind of greeting this could be. ³⁰Then the angel told her:

> Do not be afraid, Mary,
> for you have found favor with God.
> ³¹ Now listen:
> You will conceive and give birth to
>   a son,
> and you will call His name Jesus.
> ³² He will be great
> and will be called the Son of
>   the Most High,
> and the Lord God will give Him
> the throne of His father David.

A1:1 Or *events that have been accomplished*, or *events most surely believed*   B1:4 Or *informed*   C1:5 One of the 24 divisions of priests appointed by David for temple service; 1Ch 24:10   D1:7 Lit *child*   E1:7 Lit *Elizabeth was sterile* or *barren*   F1:7 Lit *in their days*   G1:12 Lit *and fear fell on him*   H1:18 Lit *in her days*   I1:28 Other mss add *blessed are you among women*

³³ He will reign over the house of Jacob
   forever,
   and His kingdom will have no end.

³⁴ Mary asked the angel, "How can this be, since I have not been intimate with a man?"ᴬ ³⁵ The angel replied to her:

   "The Holy Spirit will come upon you,
   and the power of the Most High
       will overshadow you.
   Therefore, the holy One to be born
   will be called the Son of God.

³⁶ And consider your relative Elizabeth—even she has conceived a son in her old age, and this is the sixth month for her who was called childless. ³⁷ For nothing will be impossible with God."

³⁸ "I am the Lord's slave,"ᴮ said Mary. "May it be done to me according to your word." Then the angel left her.

³⁹ In those days Mary set out and hurried to a town in the hill country of Judah ⁴⁰ where she entered Zechariah's house and greeted Elizabeth. ⁴¹ When Elizabeth heard Mary's greeting, the baby leaped inside her,ᶜ and Elizabeth was filled with the Holy Spirit. ⁴² Then she exclaimed with a loud cry:

   "You are the most blessed of women,
   and your child will be blessed!ᴰ

⁴³ How could this happen to me, that the mother of my Lord should come to me? ⁴⁴ For you see, when the sound of your greeting reached my ears, the baby leaped for joy inside me!ᴱ ⁴⁵ She who has believed is blessed because what was spoken to her by the Lord will be fulfilled!"

⁴⁶ And Mary said:

   My soul proclaims the greatness
   ofᶠ the Lord,
⁴⁷ and my spirit has rejoiced in God
   my Savior,
⁴⁸ because He has looked with favor
   on the humble condition of His slave.
   Surely, from now on all generations
   will call me blessed,
⁴⁹ because the Mighty One
   has done great things for me,
   and His name is holy.

⁵⁰ His mercy is from generation
   to generation
   on those who fear Him.
⁵¹ He has done a mighty deed
   with His arm;
   He has scattered the proud
   because of the thoughts of their hearts;
⁵² He has toppled the mighty
   from their thrones
   and exalted the lowly.
⁵³ He has satisfied the hungry
   with good things
   and sent the rich away empty.
⁵⁴ He has helped His servant Israel,
   mindful of His mercy,ᴳ
⁵⁵ just as He spoke to our ancestors,
   to Abraham and his
       descendantsᴴ forever.

⁵⁶ And Mary stayed with her about three months; then she returned to her home.

⁵⁷ Now the time had come for Elizabeth to give birth, and she had a son. ⁵⁸ Then her neighbors and relatives heard that the Lord had shown her His great mercy,ᴵ and they rejoiced with her.

⁵⁹ When they came to circumcise the child on the eighth day, they were going to name him Zechariah, after his father. ⁶⁰ But his mother responded, "No! He will be called John."

⁶¹ Then they said to her, "None of your relatives has that name." ⁶² So they motioned to his father to find out what he wanted him to be called. ⁶³ He asked for a writing tablet and wrote:

HIS NAME IS JOHN.

And they were all amazed. ⁶⁴ Immediately his mouth was opened and his tongue set free, and he began to speak, praising God. ⁶⁵ Fear came on all those who lived around them, and all these things were being talked about throughout the hill country of Judea. ⁶⁶ All who heard about him took it to heart, saying, "What then will this child become?" For, indeed, the Lord's hand was with him.

⁶⁷ Then his father Zechariah was filled with the Holy Spirit and prophesied:

⁶⁸ Praise the Lord, the God of Israel,
   because He has visited

ᴬ**1:34** Lit *since I do not know a man*   ᴮ**1:38** Lit *Look, the Lord's slave*   ᶜ**1:41** Lit *leaped in her abdomen* or *womb*   ᴰ**1:42** Lit *and the fruit of your abdomen* (or *womb*) *is blessed*   ᴱ**1:44** Lit *in my abdomen* or *womb*   ᶠ**1:46** Or *soul magnifies*   ᴳ**1:54** Because He remembered His mercy; Ps 98:3   ᴴ**1:55** Or *offspring*; lit *seed*   ᴵ**1:58** Lit *the Lord magnified His mercy with her*

and provided redemption
for His people.
⁶⁹ He has raised up a horn of salvation^A
for us
in the house of His servant David,
⁷⁰ just as He spoke by the mouth
of His holy prophets in ancient times;
⁷¹ salvation from our enemies
and from the clutches^B of those
who hate us.
⁷² He has dealt mercifully
with our fathers
and remembered His holy covenant—
⁷³ the oath that He swore to our father
Abraham.
He has given us the privilege,
⁷⁴ since we have been rescued
from our enemies' clutches,^C
to serve Him without fear
⁷⁵ in holiness and righteousness
in His presence all our days.
⁷⁶ And child, you will be called
a prophet of the Most High,
for you will go before the Lord
to prepare His ways,
⁷⁷ to give His people knowledge
of salvation
through the forgiveness of their sins.
⁷⁸ Because of our God's merciful
compassion,
the Dawn from on high will visit us
⁷⁹ to shine on those who live in darkness
and the shadow of death,
to guide our feet into the way of peace.

⁸⁰ The child grew up and became spiritually strong, and he was in the wilderness until the day of his public appearance to Israel.

2 In those days a decree went out from Caesar Augustus^D that the whole empire^E should be registered. ² This first registration took place while^F Quirinius was governing Syria. ³ So everyone went to be registered, each to his own town.

⁴ And Joseph also went up from the town of Nazareth in Galilee, to Judea, to the city of David, which is called Bethlehem, because he was of the house and family line of David, ⁵ to be registered along with Mary, who was engaged

to him^G and was pregnant. ⁶ While they were there, the time came for her to give birth. ⁷ Then she gave birth to her firstborn Son, and she wrapped Him snugly in cloth and laid Him in a feeding trough—because there was no room for them at the lodging place.

⁸ In the same region, shepherds were staying out in the fields and keeping watch at night over their flock. ⁹ Then an angel of the Lord stood before^H them, and the glory of the Lord shone around them, and they were terrified.^I ¹⁰ But the angel said to them, "Don't be afraid, for look, I proclaim to you good news of great joy that will be for all the people:^J ¹¹ Today a Savior, who is Messiah the Lord, was born for you in the city of David. ¹² This will be the sign for you: You will find a baby wrapped snugly in cloth and lying in a feeding trough."

¹³ Suddenly there was a multitude of the heavenly host with the angel, praising God and saying:

¹⁴   Glory to God in the highest heaven,
and peace on earth to people
He favors!^K,L

¹⁵ When the angels had left them and returned to heaven, the shepherds said to one another, "Let's go straight to Bethlehem and see what has happened, which the Lord has made known to us."

¹⁶ They hurried off and found both Mary and Joseph, and the baby who was lying in the feeding trough. ¹⁷ After seeing them, they reported the message they were told about this child, ¹⁸ and all who heard it were amazed at what the shepherds said to them. ¹⁹ But Mary was treasuring up all these things^M in her heart and meditating on them. ²⁰ The shepherds returned, glorifying and praising God for all they had seen and heard, just as they had been told.

²¹ When the eight days were completed for His circumcision, He was named Jesus—the name given by the angel before He was conceived.^N ²² And when the days of their purification according to the law of Moses were finished, they brought Him up to Jerusalem to present Him to the Lord ²³ (just as it is written in the law of the Lord: **Every firstborn male**^O **will be dedicated**^P **to the Lord**^Q) ²⁴ and to offer

^A1:69 = a strong Savior   ^B1:71 Lit *the hand*   ^C1:74 Lit *from the hand of enemies*   ^D2:1 Emperor who ruled the Roman Empire 27 B.C.–A.D. 14; also known as Octavian, he established the peaceful era known as the *Pax Romana*; Caesar was a title of Roman emperors.   ^E2:1 Or *the whole inhabited world*   ^F2:2 Or *This registration was the first while*, or *This registration was before*   ^G2:5 Other mss read *was his engaged wife*   ^H2:9 Or *Lord appeared to*   ^I2:9 Lit *they feared a great fear*   ^J2:10 Or *the whole nation*   ^K2:14 Other mss read *earth good will to people*   ^L2:14 Or *earth to men of good will*   ^M2:19 Lit *these words*   ^N2:21 Or *conceived in the womb*   ^O2:23 Lit *"Every male that opens a womb*   ^P2:23 Lit *be called holy*   ^Q2:23 Ex 13:2,12 a sacrifice (according to what is stated in the law of the Lord: **a pair of turtledoves or two young pigeons**[A]).

²⁵ There was a man in Jerusalem whose name was Simeon. This man was righteous and devout, looking forward to Israel's consolation,[B] and the Holy Spirit was on him. ²⁶ It had been revealed to him by the Holy Spirit that he would not see death before he saw the Lord's Messiah. ²⁷ Guided by the Spirit, he entered[C] the temple complex. When the parents brought in the child Jesus to perform for Him what was customary under the law, ²⁸ Simeon took Him up in his arms, praised God, and said:

> ²⁹ Now, Master,
> You can dismiss Your slave in peace,
> as You promised.
> ³⁰ For my eyes have seen Your salvation.
> ³¹ You have prepared it
> in the presence of all peoples—
> ³² a light for revelation to the Gentiles[D]
> and glory to Your people Israel.

³³ His father and mother[E] were amazed at what was being said about Him. ³⁴ Then Simeon blessed them and told His mother Mary: "Indeed, this child is destined to cause the fall and rise of many in Israel and to be a sign that will be opposed[F]— ³⁵ and a sword will pierce your own soul—that the thoughts[G] of many hearts may be revealed."

³⁶ There was also a prophetess, Anna, a daughter of Phanuel, of the tribe of Asher. She was well along in years,[H] having lived with her husband seven years after her marriage,[I] ³⁷ and was a widow for 84 years.[J] She did not leave the temple complex, serving God night and day with fasting and prayers. ³⁸ At that very moment,[K] she came up and began to thank God and to speak about Him to all who were looking forward to the redemption of Jerusalem.[L]

³⁹ When they had completed everything according to the law of the Lord, they returned to Galilee, to their own town of Nazareth. ⁴⁰ The boy grew up and became strong, filled with wisdom, and God's grace was on Him.

⁴¹ Every year His parents traveled to Jerusalem for the Passover Festival. ⁴² When He was 12 years old, they went up according to the custom of the festival. ⁴³ After those days were over, as they were returning, the boy Jesus stayed behind in Jerusalem, but His parents[M] did not know it. ⁴⁴ Assuming He was in the traveling party, they went a day's journey. Then they began looking for Him among their relatives and friends. ⁴⁵ When they did not find Him, they returned to Jerusalem to search for Him. ⁴⁶ After three days, they found Him in the temple complex sitting among the teachers, listening to them and asking them questions. ⁴⁷ And all those who heard Him were astounded at His understanding and His answers. ⁴⁸ When His parents saw Him, they were astonished, and His mother said to Him, "Son, why have You treated us like this? Your father and I have been anxiously searching for You."

⁴⁹ "Why were you searching for Me?" He asked them. "Didn't you know that I had to be in My Father's house?"[N] ⁵⁰ But they did not understand what He said to them.

⁵¹ Then He went down with them and came to Nazareth and was obedient to them. His mother kept all these things in her heart. ⁵² And Jesus increased in wisdom and stature, and in favor with God and with people.

3 In the fifteenth year of the reign of Tiberius Caesar,[O] while Pontius Pilate was governor of Judea, Herod was tetrarch[P] of Galilee, his brother Philip tetrarch of the region of Iturea[Q] and Trachonitis,[Q] and Lysanias tetrarch of Abilene,[R] ² during the high priesthood of Annas and Caiaphas, God's word came to John the son of Zechariah in the wilderness. ³ He went into all the vicinity of the Jordan, preaching a baptism of repentance[S] for the forgiveness of sins, ⁴ as it is written in the book of the words of the prophet Isaiah:

> **A voice of one crying out
> in the wilderness:
> Prepare the way for the Lord;
> make His paths straight!
> ⁵ Every valley will be filled,
> and every mountain and hill will be
> made low;[T]
> the crooked will become straight,
> the rough ways smooth,**

A2:24 Lv 5:11; 12:8 B2:25 The coming of the Messiah with His salvation for the nation; Is 40:1; 61:2; Lk 2:26,30 C2:27 Lit *And in the Spirit, he came into* D2:32 Or *the nations* E2:33 Other mss read *But Joseph and His mother* F2:34 Or *spoken against* G2:35 Or *schemes* H2:36 Lit *in many days* I2:36 Lit *years from her virginity* J2:37 Or *she was a widow until the age of 84* K2:38 Lit *very hour* L2:38 Other mss read *in Jerusalem* M2:43 Other mss read *but Joseph and His mother* N2:49 Or *be involved in My Father's interests* (or *things*), or *be among My Father's people* O3:1 Emperor who ruled the Roman Empire A.D. 14–37 P3:1 Or *ruler* Q3:1 A small province northeast of Galilee R3:1 A small Syrian province S3:3 Or *baptism based on repentance* T3:5 Lit *be humbled*

⁶ **and everyone**ᴬ **will see the salvation of God.**ᴮ

⁷He then said to the crowds who came out to be baptized by him, "Brood of vipers! Who warned you to flee from the coming wrath? ⁸Therefore produce fruit consistent with repentance. And don't start saying to yourselves, 'We have Abraham as our father,' for I tell you that God is able to raise up children for Abraham from these stones! ⁹Even now the ax is ready to strikeᶜ the root of the trees! Therefore, every tree that doesn't produce good fruit will be cut down and thrown into the fire."

¹⁰"What then should we do?" the crowds were asking him.

¹¹He replied to them, "The one who has two shirtsᴰ must share with someone who has none, and the one who has food must do the same."

¹²Tax collectors also came to be baptized, and they asked him, "Teacher, what should we do?"

¹³He told them, "Don't collect any more than what you have been authorized."

¹⁴Some soldiers also questioned him: "What should we do?"

He said to them, "Don't take money from anyone by force or false accusation; be satisfied with your wages."

¹⁵Now the people were waiting expectantly, and all of them were debating in their mindsᴱ whether John might be the Messiah. ¹⁶John answered them all, "I baptize you withᶠ water, but One is coming who is more powerful than I. I am not worthy to untie the strap of His sandals. He will baptize you withᶠ the Holy Spirit and fire. ¹⁷His winnowing shovelᴳ is in His hand to clear His threshing floor and gather the wheat into His barn, but the chaff He will burn up with a fire that never goes out." ¹⁸Then, along with many other exhortations, he proclaimed good news to the people. ¹⁹But Herod the tetrarch, being rebuked by him about Herodias, his brother's wife, and about all the evil things Herod had done, ²⁰added this to everything else—he locked John up in prison.

²¹When all the people were baptized, Jesus also was baptized. As He was praying, heaven opened, ²²and the Holy Spirit descended on

Him in a physical appearance like a dove. And a voice came from heaven:

> You are My beloved Son.
> I take delight in You!

²³As He began His ministry, Jesus was about 30 years old and was thought to beᴴ the

son of Joseph, sonᴵ of Heli,
²⁴ son of Matthat, son of Levi,
son of Melchi, son of Jannai,
son of Joseph, ²⁵son of Mattathias,
son of Amos, son of Nahum,
son of Esli, son of Naggai,
²⁶ son of Maath, son of Mattathias,
son of Semein, son of Josech,
son of Joda, ²⁷son of Joanan,
son of Rhesa, son of Zerubbabel,
son of Shealtiel, son of Neri,
²⁸ son of Melchi, son of Addi,
son of Cosam, son of Elmadam,
son of Er, ²⁹son of Joshua,
son of Eliezer, son of Jorim,
son of Matthat, son of Levi,
³⁰ son of Simeon, son of Judah,
son of Joseph, son of Jonam,
son of Eliakim, ³¹son of Melea,
son of Menna, son of Mattatha,
son of Nathan, son of David,
³² son of Jesse, son of Obed,
son of Boaz, son of Salmon,ᴶ
son of Nahshon, ³³son of Amminadab,
son of Ram,ᴷ son of Hezron,
son of Perez, son of Judah,
³⁴ son of Jacob, son of Isaac,
son of Abraham, son of Terah,
son of Nahor, ³⁵son of Serug,
son of Reu, son of Peleg,
son of Eber, son of Shelah,
³⁶ son of Cainan, son of Arphaxad,
son of Shem, son of Noah,
son of Lamech, ³⁷son of Methuselah,
son of Enoch, son of Jared,
son of Mahalaleel, son of Cainan,
³⁸ son of Enos, son of Seth,
son of Adam, son of God.

4 Then Jesus returned from the Jordan, full of the Holy Spirit, and was led by the Spirit in the wilderness ²for 40 days to be tempted by the Devil. He ate nothing during those days,

ᴬ**3:6** Lit *all flesh* ᴮ**3:4-6** Is 40:3-5 ᶜ**3:9** Lit *the ax lies at* ᴰ**3:11** Lit *tunics* ᴱ**3:15** Or *hearts* ᶠ**3:16** Or *in* ᴳ**3:17** A wooden farm implement used to toss threshed grain into the wind so the lighter chaff would blow away and separate from the heavier grain ᴴ**3:23** People did not know about His virgin birth; Mt 1:18-25; Lk 1:26-38 ᴵ**3:23** The relationship in some cases may be more distant than a son. ᴶ**3:32** Other mss read *Sala* ᴷ**3:33** Other mss read *Amminadab, son of Aram, son of Joram*; other mss read *Amminadab, son of Admin, son of Arni* and when they were over,[A] He was hungry. [3]The Devil said to Him, "If You are the Son of God, tell this stone to become bread."

[4]But Jesus answered him, "It is written: **Man must not live on bread alone."[B,C]**

[5]So he took Him up[D] and showed Him all the kingdoms of the world in a moment of time. [6]The Devil said to Him, "I will give You their splendor and all this authority, because it has been given over to me, and I can give it to anyone I want. [7]If You, then, will worship me,[E] all will be Yours."

[8]And Jesus answered him,[F] "It is written:

> Worship the Lord your God,
> and serve Him only."[G]

[9]So he took Him to Jerusalem, had Him stand on the pinnacle of the temple, and said to Him, "If You are the Son of God, throw Yourself down from here. [10]For it is written:

> **He will give His angels orders
> concerning you,
> to protect you,[H] [11]and
> they will support you with their hands,
> so that you will not strike
> your foot against a stone."[I]**

[12]And Jesus answered him, "It is said: **Do not test the Lord your God."[J]**

[13]After the Devil had finished every temptation, he departed from Him for a time.

[14]Then Jesus returned to Galilee in the power of the Spirit, and news about Him spread throughout the entire vicinity. [15]He was teaching in their synagogues, being acclaimed[K] by everyone.

[16]He came to Nazareth, where He had been brought up. As usual, He entered the synagogue on the Sabbath day and stood up to read. [17]The scroll of the prophet Isaiah was given to Him, and unrolling the scroll, He found the place where it was written:

[18] The Spirit of the Lord is on Me,
because He has anointed Me
to preach good news to the poor.
He has sent Me[L]
to proclaim freedom[M] to the captives
and recovery of sight to the blind,
to set free the oppressed,

[19] to proclaim the year
of the Lord's favor.[N,O]

[20]He then rolled up the scroll, gave it back to the attendant, and sat down. And the eyes of everyone in the synagogue were fixed on Him. [21]He began by saying to them, "Today as you listen, this Scripture has been fulfilled."

[22]They were all speaking well of Him[P] and were amazed by the gracious words that came from His mouth, yet they said, "Isn't this Joseph's son?"

[23]Then He said to them, "No doubt you will quote this proverb[Q] to Me: 'Doctor, heal yourself. So all we've heard that took place in Capernaum, do here in Your hometown also.'"

[24]He also said, "I assure you: No prophet is accepted in his hometown. [25]But I say to you, there were certainly many widows in Israel in Elijah's days, when the sky was shut up for three years and six months while a great famine came over all the land. [26]Yet Elijah was not sent to any of them—but to a widow at Zarephath in Sidon. [27]And in the prophet Elisha's time, there were many in Israel who had serious skin diseases, yet not one of them was healed[R]—only Naaman the Syrian."

[28]When they heard this, everyone in the synagogue was enraged. [29]They got up, drove Him out of town, and brought Him to the edge[S] of the hill that their town was built on, intending to hurl Him over the cliff. [30]But He passed right through the crowd and went on His way.

[31]Then He went down to Capernaum, a town in Galilee, and was teaching them on the Sabbath. [32]They were astonished at His teaching because His message had authority. [33]In the synagogue there was a man with an unclean demonic spirit who cried out with a loud voice, [34]"Leave us alone![T] What do You have to do with us,[U] Jesus—Nazarene? Have You come to destroy us? I know who You are—the Holy One of God!"

[35]But Jesus rebuked him and said, "Be quiet and come out of him!"

And throwing him down before them, the demon came out of him without hurting him at all. [36]Amazement came over them all, and they kept saying to one another, "What is this message? For He commands the unclean spirits with authority and power, and they come out!" [37] And news about Him began to go out to every place in the vicinity.

[38] After He left the synagogue, He entered Simon's house. Simon's mother-in-law was suffering from a high fever, and they asked Him about her. [39] So He stood over her and rebuked the fever, and it left her. She got up immediately and began to serve them.

[40] When the sun was setting, all those who had anyone sick with various diseases brought them to Him. As He laid His hands on each one of them, He would heal them. [41] Also, demons were coming out of many, shouting and saying, "You are the Son of God!" But He rebuked them and would not allow them to speak, because they knew He was the Messiah.

[42] When it was day, He went out and made His way to a deserted place. But the crowds were searching for Him. They came to Him and tried to keep Him from leaving them. [43] But He said to them, "I must proclaim the good news about the kingdom of God to the other towns also, because I was sent for this purpose." [44] And He was preaching in the synagogues of Galilee.[A]

5 As the crowd was pressing in on Jesus to hear God's word, He was standing by Lake Gennesaret.[B] [2] He saw two boats at the edge of the lake;[C] the fishermen had left them and were washing their nets. [3] He got into one of the boats, which belonged to Simon, and asked him to put out a little from the land. Then He sat down and was teaching the crowds from the boat.

[4] When He had finished speaking, He said to Simon, "Put out into deep water and let down[D] your nets for a catch."

[5] "Master," Simon replied, "we've worked hard all night long and caught nothing! But at Your word, I'll let down the nets."[E]

[6] When they did this, they caught a great number of fish, and their nets[E] began to tear. [7] So they signaled to their partners in the other boat to come and help them; they came and filled both boats so full that they began to sink.

[8] When Simon Peter saw this, he fell at Jesus' knees and said, "Go away from me, because I'm a sinful man, Lord!" [9] For he and all those with him were amazed[F] at the catch of fish they took, [10] and so were James and John, Zebedee's sons, who were Simon's partners.

"Don't be afraid," Jesus told Simon. "From now on you will be catching people!" [11] Then they brought the boats to land, left everything, and followed Him.

[12] While He was in one of the towns, a man was there who had a serious skin disease all over him. He saw Jesus, fell facedown, and begged Him: "Lord, if You are willing, You can make me clean."

[13] Reaching out His hand, He touched him, saying, "I am willing; be made clean," and immediately the disease left him. [14] Then He ordered him to tell no one: "But go and show yourself to the priest, and offer what Moses prescribed for your cleansing as a testimony to them."

[15] But the news[G] about Him spread even more, and large crowds would come together to hear Him and to be healed of their sicknesses. [16] Yet He often withdrew to deserted places and prayed.

[17] On one of those days while He was teaching, Pharisees and teachers of the law were sitting there who had come from every village of Galilee and Judea, and also from Jerusalem. And the Lord's power to heal was in Him. [18] Just then some men came, carrying on a mat a man who was paralyzed. They tried to bring him in and set him down before Him. [19] Since they could not find a way to bring him in because of the crowd, they went up on the roof and lowered him on the mat through the roof tiles into the middle of the crowd before Jesus.

[20] Seeing their faith He said, "Friend,[H] your sins are forgiven you."

[21] Then the scribes and the Pharisees began to think: "Who is this man who speaks blasphemies? Who can forgive sins but God alone?"

[22] But perceiving their thoughts, Jesus replied to them, "Why are you thinking this in your hearts?[I] [23] Which is easier: to say, 'Your sins are forgiven you,' or to say, 'Get up and walk'? [24] But so you may know that the Son of Man has authority on earth to forgive sins"—He told the paralyzed man, "I tell you: Get up, pick up your mat, and go home."

[25] Immediately he got up before them, picked up what he had been lying on, and went home glorifying God. [26] Then everyone was astounded, and they were giving glory to God.

And they were filled with awe and said, "We have seen incredible things today!"

²⁷After this, Jesus went out and saw a tax collector named Levi sitting at the tax office, and He said to him, "Follow Me!" ²⁸So, leaving everything behind, he got up and began to follow Him.

²⁹Then Levi hosted a grand banquet for Him at his house. Now there was a large crowd of tax collectors and others who were guestsᴬ with them. ³⁰But the Pharisees and their scribes were complaining to His disciples, "Why do you eat and drink with tax collectors and sinners?"

³¹Jesus replied to them, "The healthy don't need a doctor, but the sick do. ³²I have not come to call the righteous, but sinners to repentance."

³³Then they said to Him, "John's disciples fast often and say prayers, and those of the Pharisees do the same, but Yours eat and drink."ᴮ

³⁴Jesus said to them, "You can't make the wedding guestsᶜ fast while the groom is with them, can you? ³⁵But the timeᴰ will come when the groom will be taken away from them—then they will fast in those days."

³⁶He also told them a parable: "No one tears a patch from a new garment and puts it on an old garment. Otherwise, not only will he tear the new, but also the piece from the new garment will not match the old. ³⁷And no one puts new wine into old wineskins. Otherwise, the new wine will burst the skins, it will spill, and the skins will be ruined. ³⁸But new wine should be put into fresh wineskins.ᴱ ³⁹And no one, after drinking old wine, wants new, because he says, 'The old is better.'"ᶠ

6 On a Sabbath,⁶ He passed through the grainfields. His disciples were picking heads of grain, rubbing them in their hands, and eating them. ²But some of the Pharisees said, "Why are you doing what is not lawful on the Sabbath?"

³Jesus answered them, "Haven't you read what David and those who were with him did when he was hungry— ⁴how he entered the house of God, and took and ate the sacred bread, which is not lawful for any but the priests to eat? He even gave some to those who

were with him." ⁵Then He told them, "The Son of Man is Lord of the Sabbath."

⁶On another Sabbath He entered the synagogue and was teaching. A man was there whose right hand was paralyzed. ⁷The scribes and Pharisees were watching Him closely, to see if He would heal on the Sabbath, so that they could find a charge against Him. ⁸But He knew their thoughts and told the man with the paralyzed hand, "Get up and stand here."ᴴ So he got up and stood there. ⁹Then Jesus said to them, "I ask you: Is it lawful on the Sabbath to do what is good or to do what is evil, to save life or to destroy it?" ¹⁰After looking around at them all, He told him, "Stretch out your hand." He did so, and his hand was restored.ᴵ ¹¹They, however, were filled with rage and started discussing with one another what they might do to Jesus.

¹²During those days He went out to the mountain to pray and spent all night in prayer to God. ¹³When daylight came, He summoned His disciples, and He chose 12 of them—He also named them apostles:

14 Simon, whom He also named Peter,
and Andrew his brother;
James and John;
Philip and Bartholomew;
15 Matthew and Thomas;
James the son of Alphaeus,
and Simon called the Zealot;
16 Judas the son of James,
and Judas Iscariot, who became
a traitor.

¹⁷After coming down with them, He stood on a level place with a large crowd of His disciples and a great number of people from all Judea and Jerusalem and from the seacoast of Tyre and Sidon. ¹⁸They came to hear Him and to be healed of their diseases; and those tormented by unclean spirits were made well. ¹⁹The whole crowd was trying to touch Him, because power was coming out from Him and healing them all.

²⁰Then looking up atᴶ His disciples, He said:

You who are poor are blessed,
because the kingdom of God is yours.
21 You who are now hungry are blessed,

because you will be filled.
You who now weep are blessed,
because you will laugh.
²² You are blessed when people hate you,
when they exclude you, insult you,
and slander your name as evil
because of the Son of Man.

²³ "Rejoice in that day and leap for joy! Take note—your reward is great in heaven, for this is the way their ancestors used to treat the prophets.

²⁴ But woe to you who are rich,
for you have received your comfort.
²⁵ Woe to you who are now full,
for you will be hungry.
Woe to you^A who are now laughing,
for you will mourn and weep.
²⁶ Woe to you^A
when all people speak well of you,
for this is the way their ancestors
used to treat the false prophets.

²⁷ "But I say to you who listen: Love your enemies, do what is good to those who hate you, ²⁸ bless those who curse you, pray for those who mistreat you. ²⁹ If anyone hits you on the cheek, offer the other also. And if anyone takes away your coat, don't hold back your shirt either. ³⁰ Give to everyone who asks you, and from one who takes your things, don't ask for them back. ³¹ Just as you want others to do for you, do the same for them. ³² If you love those who love you, what credit is that to you? Even sinners love those who love them. ³³ If you do what is good to those who are good to you, what credit is that to you? Even sinners do that. ³⁴ And if you lend to those from whom you expect to receive, what credit is that to you? Even sinners lend to sinners to be repaid in full. ³⁵ But love your enemies, do what is good, and lend, expecting nothing in return. Then your reward will be great, and you will be sons of the Most High. For He is gracious to the ungrateful and evil. ³⁶ Be merciful, just as your Father also is merciful.

³⁷ "Do not judge, and you will not be judged. Do not condemn, and you will not be condemned. Forgive, and you will be forgiven. ³⁸ Give, and it will be given to you; a good measure—pressed down, shaken together, and running over—will be poured into your lap.

For with the measure you use,^B it will be measured back to you."

³⁹ He also told them a parable: "Can the blind guide the blind? Won't they both fall into a pit? ⁴⁰ A disciple is not above his teacher, but everyone who is fully trained will be like his teacher.

⁴¹ "Why do you look at the speck in your brother's eye, but don't notice the log in your own eye? ⁴² Or how can you say to your brother, 'Brother, let me take out the speck that is in your eye,' when you yourself don't see the log in your eye? Hypocrite! First take the log out of your eye, and then you will see clearly to take out the speck in your brother's eye.

⁴³ "A good tree doesn't produce bad fruit; on the other hand, a bad tree doesn't produce good fruit. ⁴⁴ For each tree is known by its own fruit. Figs aren't gathered from thornbushes, or grapes picked from a bramble bush. ⁴⁵ A good man produces good out of the good storeroom of his heart. An evil man produces evil out of the evil storeroom, for his mouth speaks from the overflow of the heart.

⁴⁶ "Why do you call Me 'Lord, Lord,' and don't do the things I say? ⁴⁷ I will show you what someone is like who comes to Me, hears My words, and acts on them: ⁴⁸ He is like a man building a house, who dug deep^C and laid the foundation on the rock. When the flood came, the river crashed against that house and couldn't shake it, because it was well built. ⁴⁹ But the one who hears and does not act is like a man who built a house on the ground without a foundation. The river crashed against it, and immediately it collapsed. And the destruction of that house was great!"

7 When He had concluded all His sayings in the hearing of the people, He entered Capernaum. ² A centurion's slave, who was highly valued by him, was sick and about to die. ³ When the centurion heard about Jesus, he sent some Jewish elders to Him, requesting Him to come and save the life of his slave. ⁴ When they reached Jesus, they pleaded with Him earnestly, saying, "He is worthy for You to grant this, ⁵ because he loves our nation and has built us a synagogue." ⁶ Jesus went with them, and when He was not far from^D the house, the centurion sent friends to tell Him, "Lord, don't trouble Yourself, since I am not worthy to have You come under my roof. ⁷ That is why I didn't even consider myself worthy to

^A6:25,26 Other mss omit *to you*   ^B6:38 Lit *you measure*   ^C6:48 Lit *dug and went deep*   ^D7:6 Lit *and He already was not far from*

come to You. But say the word, and my servant will be cured.[A] [8]For I too am a man placed under authority, having soldiers under my command.[B] I say to this one, 'Go!' and he goes; and to another, 'Come!' and he comes; and to my slave, 'Do this!' and he does it."

[9]Jesus heard this and was amazed at him, and turning to the crowd following Him, He said, "I tell you, I have not found so great a faith even in Israel!" [10]When those who had been sent returned to the house, they found the slave in good health.

[11]Soon afterward He was on His way to a town called Nain. His disciples and a large crowd were traveling with Him. [12]Just as He neared the gate of the town, a dead man was being carried out. He was his mother's only son, and she was a widow. A large crowd from the city was also with her. [13]When the Lord saw her, He had compassion on her and said, "Don't cry." [14]Then He came up and touched the open coffin,[C] and the pallbearers stopped. And He said, "Young man, I tell you, get up!"

[15]The dead man sat up and began to speak, and Jesus gave him to his mother. [16]Then fear[D] came over everyone, and they glorified God, saying, "A great prophet has risen among us," and "God has visited[E] His people." [17]This report about Him went throughout Judea and all the vicinity.

[18]Then John's disciples told him about all these things. So John summoned two of his disciples [19]and sent them to the Lord, asking, "Are You the One who is to come, or should we look for someone else?"

[20]When the men reached Him, they said, "John the Baptist sent us to ask You, 'Are You the One who is to come, or should we look for someone else?'"

[21]At that time Jesus healed many people of diseases, plagues, and evil spirits, and He granted sight to many blind people. [22]He replied to them, "Go and report to John the things you have seen and heard: The blind receive their sight, the lame walk, those with skin diseases are healed,[F] the deaf hear, the dead are raised, and the poor are told the good news. [23]And anyone who is not offended because of Me is blessed." [24]After John's messengers left, He began to speak to the crowds about John: "What did you go out into the wilderness to see? A reed swaying in the wind? [25]What then did you go out to see? A man dressed in soft robes? Look, those who are splendidly dressed[G] and live in luxury are in royal palaces. [26]What then did you go out to see? A prophet? Yes, I tell you, and far more than a prophet. [27]This is the one it is written about:

> Look, I am sending My messenger
> ahead of You;[H]
> he will prepare Your way before You.[I]

[28]I tell you, among those born of women no one is greater than John,[J] but the least in the kingdom of God is greater than he."

[29](And when all the people, including the tax collectors, heard this, they acknowledged God's way of righteousness,[K] because they had been baptized with John's baptism. [30]But since the Pharisees and experts in the law had not been baptized by him, they rejected the plan of God for themselves.)

[31]"To what then should I compare the people of this generation, and what are they like? [32]They are like children sitting in the marketplace and calling to each other:

> We played the flute for you,
> but you didn't dance;
> we sang a lament,
> but you didn't weep!

[33]For John the Baptist did not come eating bread or drinking wine, and you say, 'He has a demon!' [34]The Son of Man has come eating and drinking, and you say, 'Look, a glutton and a drunkard, a friend of tax collectors and sinners!' [35]Yet wisdom is vindicated[L] by all her children."

[36]Then one of the Pharisees invited Him to eat with him. He entered the Pharisee's house and reclined at the table. [37]And a woman in the town who was a sinner found out that Jesus was reclining at the table in the Pharisee's house. She brought an alabaster jar of fragrant oil [38]and stood behind Him at His feet, weeping, and began to wash His feet with her tears. She wiped His feet with the hair of her head, kissing them and anointing them with the fragrant oil.

[39]When the Pharisee who had invited Him saw this, he said to himself, "This man, if He were a prophet, would know who and

---

[A]**7:7** Other mss read *and let my servant be cured*   [B]**7:8** Lit *under me*   [C]**7:14** Or *the bier*   [D]**7:16** Or *awe*   [E]**7:16** Or *come to help*   [F]**7:22** Lit *cleansed*   [G]**7:25** Or *who have glorious robes*   [H]**7:27** Lit *messenger before Your face*   [I]**7:27** Mal 3:1   [J]**7:28** Other mss read *women is not a greater prophet than John the Baptist*   [K]**7:29** Lit *they justified God*   [L]**7:35** Or *wisdom is declared right* what kind of woman this is who is touching Him—she's a sinner!"

⁴⁰Jesus replied to him, "Simon, I have something to say to you."

"Teacher," he said, "say it."

⁴¹"A creditor had two debtors. One owed 500 denarii, and the other 50. ⁴²Since they could not pay it back, he graciously forgave them both. So, which of them will love him more?"

⁴³Simon answered, "I suppose the one he forgave more."

"You have judged correctly," He told him. ⁴⁴Turning to the woman, He said to Simon, "Do you see this woman? I entered your house; you gave Me no water for My feet, but she, with her tears, has washed My feet and wiped them with her hair. ⁴⁵You gave Me no kiss, but she hasn't stopped kissing My feet since I came in. ⁴⁶You didn't anoint My head with olive oil, but she has anointed My feet with fragrant oil. ⁴⁷Therefore I tell you, her many sins have been forgiven; that's whyᴬ she loved much. But the one who is forgiven little, loves little." ⁴⁸Then He said to her, "Your sins are forgiven."

⁴⁹Those who were at the table with Him began to say among themselves, "Who is this man who even forgives sins?"

⁵⁰And He said to the woman, "Your faith has saved you. Go in peace."

8 Soon afterward He was traveling from one town and village to another, preaching and telling the good news of the kingdom of God. The Twelve were with Him, ²and also some women who had been healed of evil spirits and sicknesses: Mary, called Magdalene (seven demons had come out of her); ³Joanna the wife of Chuza, Herod's steward; Susanna; and many others who were supporting them from their possessions.

⁴As a large crowd was gathering, and people were flocking to Him from every town, He said in a parable: ⁵"A sower went out to sow his seed. As he was sowing, some fell along the path; it was trampled on, and the birds of the sky ate it up. ⁶Other seed fell on the rock; when it sprang up, it withered, since it lacked moisture. ⁷Other seed fell among thorns; the thorns sprang up with it and choked it. ⁸Still other seed fell on good ground; when it sprang up, it produced a crop: 100 times what was sown." As He said this, He called out, "Anyone who has ears to hear should listen!"

⁹Then His disciples asked Him, "What does this parable mean?" ¹⁰So He said, "The secrets of the kingdom of God have been given for you to know, but to the rest it is in parables, so that

> Looking they may not see,
> and hearing they may not understand.ᴮ

¹¹"This is the meaning of the parable:ᶜ The seed is the word of God. ¹²The seed along the path are those who have heard and then the Devil comes and takes away the word from their hearts, so that they may not believe and be saved. ¹³And the seed on the rock are those who, when they hear, welcome the word with joy. Having no root, these believe for a while and depart in a time of testing. ¹⁴As for the seed that fell among thorns, these are the ones who, when they have heard, go on their way and are choked with worries, riches, and pleasures of life, and produce no mature fruit. ¹⁵But the seed in the good ground—these are the ones who,ᴰ having heard the word with an honest and good heart, hold on to it and by enduring, bear fruit.

¹⁶"No one, after lighting a lamp, covers it with a basket or puts it under a bed, but puts it on a lampstand so that those who come in may see its light. ¹⁷For nothing is concealed that won't be revealed, and nothing hidden that won't be made known and come to light. ¹⁸Therefore take care how you listen. For whoever has, more will be given to him; and whoever does not have, even what he thinks he has will be taken away from him."

¹⁹Then His mother and brothers came to Him, but they could not meet with Him because of the crowd. ²⁰He was told, "Your mother and Your brothers are standing outside, wanting to see You."

²¹But He replied to them, "My mother and My brothers are those who hear and do the word of God."

²²One day He and His disciples got into a boat, and He told them, "Let's cross over to the other side of the lake." So they set out, ²³and as they were sailing He fell asleep. Then a fierce windstorm came down on the lake; they were being swamped and were in danger. ²⁴They came and woke Him up, saying, "Master, Master, we're going to die!" Then He got up and rebuked the wind and the raging waves. So

they ceased, and there was a calm. [25] He said to them, "Where is your faith?"

They were fearful and amazed, asking one another, "Who can this be?[A] He commands even the winds and the waves, and they obey Him!"

[26] Then they sailed to the region of the Gerasenes,[B] which is opposite Galilee. [27] When He got out on land, a demon-possessed man from the town met Him. For a long time he had worn no clothes and did not stay in a house but in the tombs. [28] When he saw Jesus, he cried out, fell down before Him, and said in a loud voice, "What do You have to do with me,[C] Jesus, You Son of the Most High God? I beg You, don't torment me!" [29] For He had commanded the unclean spirit to come out of the man. Many times it had seized him, and though he was guarded, bound by chains and shackles, he would snap the restraints and be driven by the demon into deserted places.

[30] "What is your name?" Jesus asked him.

"Legion," he said—because many demons had entered him. [31] And they begged Him not to banish them to the abyss.

[32] A large herd of pigs was there, feeding on the hillside. The demons begged Him to permit them to enter the pigs, and He gave them permission. [33] The demons came out of the man and entered the pigs, and the herd rushed down the steep bank into the lake and drowned. [34] When the men who tended them saw what had happened, they ran off and reported it in the town and in the countryside. [35] Then people went out to see what had happened. They came to Jesus and found the man the demons had departed from, sitting at Jesus' feet, dressed and in his right mind. And they were afraid. [36] Meanwhile, the eyewitnesses reported to them how the demon-possessed man was delivered. [37] Then all the people of the Gerasene region[B] asked Him to leave them, because they were gripped by great fear. So getting into the boat, He returned.

[38] The man from whom the demons had departed kept begging to be with Him. But He sent him away and said, [39] "Go back to your home, and tell all that God has done for you." And off he went, proclaiming throughout the town all that Jesus had done for him.

[40] When Jesus returned, the crowd welcomed Him, for they were all expecting Him. [41] Just then, a man named Jairus came. He was a leader of the synagogue. He fell down at Jesus' feet and pleaded with Him to come to his house, [42] because he had an only daughter about 12 years old, and she was at death's door.[D]

While He was going, the crowds were nearly crushing Him. [43] A woman suffering from bleeding for 12 years, who had spent all she had on doctors[E] yet could not be healed by any, [44] approached from behind and touched the tassel of His robe. Instantly her bleeding stopped.

[45] "Who touched Me?" Jesus asked.

When they all denied it, Peter[F] said, "Master, the crowds are hemming You in and pressing against You."[G]

[46] "Someone did touch Me," said Jesus. "I know that power has gone out from Me." [47] When the woman saw that she was discovered,[H] she came trembling and fell down before Him. In the presence of all the people, she declared the reason she had touched Him and how she was instantly cured. [48] "Daughter," He said to her, "your faith has made you well.[I] Go in peace."

[49] While He was still speaking, someone came from the synagogue leader's house, saying, "Your daughter is dead. Don't bother the Teacher anymore."

[50] When Jesus heard it, He answered him, "Don't be afraid. Only believe, and she will be made well." [51] After He came to the house, He let no one enter with Him except Peter, John, James, and the child's father and mother. [52] Everyone was crying and mourning for her. But He said, "Stop crying, for she is not dead but asleep."

[53] They started laughing at Him, because they knew she was dead. [54] So He[J] took her by the hand and called out, "Child, get up!" [55] Her spirit returned, and she got up at once. Then He gave orders that she be given something to eat. [56] Her parents were astounded, but He instructed them to tell no one what had happened.

9 Summoning the Twelve, He gave them power and authority over all the demons, and power to heal[K] diseases. [2] Then He sent

A8:25 Lit *Who then is this?* B8:26,37 Other mss read *the Gadarenes* C8:28 Lit *What to me and to You* D8:42 Lit *she was dying* E8:43 Other mss omit *who had spent all she had on doctors* F8:45 Other mss add *and those with him* G8:45 Other mss add *and You say, 'Who touched Me?'* H8:47 Lit *she had not escaped notice* I8:48 Or *has saved you* J8:54 Other mss add *having put them all outside* K9:1 In this passage, different Gk words are translated as heal. In Eng, "to heal" or "to cure" are synonyms with little distinction in meaning. Technically, we do not heal or cure diseases. People are healed or cured from diseases.

them to proclaim the kingdom of God and to heal the sick.

3 "Take nothing for the road," He told them, "no walking stick, no traveling bag, no bread, no money; and don't take an extra shirt. 4 Whatever house you enter, stay there and leave from there. 5 If they do not welcome you, when you leave that town, shake off the dust from your feet as a testimony against them." 6 So they went out and traveled from village to village, proclaiming the good news and healing everywhere.

7 Herod the tetrarch heard about everything that was going on. He was perplexed, because some said that John had been raised from the dead, 8 some that Elijah had appeared, and others that one of the ancient prophets had risen. 9 "I beheaded John," Herod said, "but who is this I hear such things about?" And he wanted to see Him.

10 When the apostles returned, they reported to Jesus all that they had done. He took them along and withdrew privately to a[A] town called Bethsaida. 11 When the crowds found out, they followed Him. He welcomed them, spoke to them about the kingdom of God, and cured[B] those who needed healing.

12 Late in the day,[C] the Twelve approached and said to Him, "Send the crowd away, so they can go into the surrounding villages and countryside to find food and lodging, because we are in a deserted place here."

13 "You give them something to eat," He told them.

"We have no more than five loaves and two fish," they said, "unless we go and buy food for all these people." 14 (For about 5,000 men were there.)

Then He told His disciples, "Have them sit down[D] in groups of about 50 each." 15 They did so, and had them all sit down. 16 Then He took the five loaves and the two fish, and looking up to heaven, He blessed and broke them. He kept giving them to the disciples to set before the crowd. 17 Everyone ate and was filled. Then they picked up[E] 12 baskets of leftover pieces.

18 While He was praying in private and His disciples were with Him, He asked them, "Who do the crowds say that I am?"

19 They answered, "John the Baptist; others, Elijah; still others, that one of the ancient prophets has come back."[F]

20 "But you," He asked them, "who do you say that I am?"

Peter answered, "God's Messiah!"

21 But He strictly warned and instructed them to tell this to no one, 22 saying, "The Son of Man must suffer many things and be rejected by the elders, chief priests, and scribes, be killed, and be raised the third day."

23 Then He said to them all, "If anyone wants to come with[G] Me, he must deny himself, take up his cross daily,[H] and follow Me. 24 For whoever wants to save his life will lose it, but whoever loses his life because of Me will save it. 25 What is a man benefited if he gains the whole world, yet loses or forfeits himself? 26 For whoever is ashamed of Me and My words, the Son of Man will be ashamed of him when He comes in His glory and that of the Father and the holy angels. 27 I tell you the truth: There are some standing here who will not taste death until they see the kingdom of God."

28 About eight days after these words, He took along Peter, John, and James and went up on the mountain to pray. 29 As He was praying, the appearance of His face changed, and His clothes became dazzling white. 30 Suddenly, two men were talking with Him—Moses and Elijah. 31 They appeared in glory and were speaking of His death,[I] which He was about to accomplish in Jerusalem.

32 Peter and those with him were in a deep sleep,[J] and when they became fully awake, they saw His glory and the two men who were standing with Him. 33 As the two men were departing from Him, Peter said to Jesus, "Master, it's good for us to be here! Let us make three tabernacles: one for You, one for Moses, and one for Elijah"—not knowing what he said.

34 While he was saying this, a cloud appeared and overshadowed them. They became afraid as they entered the cloud. 35 Then a voice came from the cloud, saying:

This is My Son, the Chosen One;[K]
listen to Him!

³⁶After the voice had spoken, only Jesus was found. They kept silent, and in those days told no one what they had seen.

³⁷The next day, when they came down from the mountain, a large crowd met Him. ³⁸Just then a man from the crowd cried out, "Teacher, I beg You to look at my son, because he's my only child. ³⁹Often a spirit seizes him; suddenly he shrieks, and it throws him into convulsions until he foams at the mouth;ᴬ woundingᴮ him, it hardly ever leaves him. ⁴⁰I begged Your disciples to drive it out, but they couldn't."

⁴¹Jesus replied, "You unbelieving and rebelliousᶜ generation! How long will I be with you and put up with you? Bring your son here."

⁴²As the boy was still approaching, the demon knocked him down and threw him into severe convulsions. But Jesus rebuked the unclean spirit, cured the boy, and gave him back to his father. ⁴³And they were all astonished at the greatness of God.

While everyone was amazed at all the things He was doing, He told His disciples, ⁴⁴"Let these words sink in:ᴰ The Son of Man is about to be betrayed into the hands of men."

⁴⁵But they did not understand this statement; it was concealed from them so that they could not grasp it, and they were afraid to ask Him about it.ᴱ

⁴⁶Then an argument started among them about who would be the greatest of them. ⁴⁷But Jesus, knowing the thoughts of their hearts, took a little child and had him stand next to Him. ⁴⁸He told them, "Whoever welcomesᶠ this little child in My name welcomes Me. And whoever welcomes Me welcomes Him who sent Me. For whoever is least among you—this one is great."

⁴⁹John responded, "Master, we saw someone driving out demons in Your name, and we tried to stop him because he does not follow us."

⁵⁰"Don't stop him," Jesus told him, "because whoever is not against you is for you."ᴳ

⁵¹When the days were coming to a close for Him to be taken up,ᴴ He determinedᴵ to journey to Jerusalem. ⁵²He sent messengers ahead of Him, and on the way they entered a village of the Samaritans to make preparations for

Him. ⁵³But they did not welcome Him, because He determined to journey to Jerusalem. ⁵⁴When the disciples James and John saw this, they said, "Lord, do You want us to call down fire from heaven to consume them?"ᴶ

⁵⁵But He turned and rebuked them,ᴷ ⁵⁶and they went to another village.

⁵⁷As they were traveling on the road someone said to Him, "I will follow You wherever You go!"

⁵⁸Jesus told him, "Foxes have dens, and birds of the skyᴸ have nests, but the Son of Man has no place to lay His head." ⁵⁹Then He said to another, "Follow Me."

"Lord," he said, "first let me go bury my father."ᴹ

⁶⁰But He told him, "Let the dead bury their own dead, but you go and spread the news of the kingdom of God."

⁶¹Another also said, "I will follow You, Lord, but first let me go and say good-bye to those at my house."

⁶²But Jesus said to him, "No one who puts his hand to the plow and looks back is fit for the kingdom of God."

10 After this, the Lord appointed 70ᴺ others, and He sent them ahead of Him in pairs to every town and place where He Himself was about to go. ²He told them: "The harvest is abundant, but the workers are few. Therefore, pray to the Lord of the harvest to send out workers into His harvest. ³Now go; I'm sending you out like lambs among wolves. ⁴Don't carry a money-bag, traveling bag, or sandals; don't greet anyone along the road. ⁵Whatever house you enter, first say, 'Peace to this household.' ⁶If a son of peaceᴼ is there, your peace will rest on him; but if not, it will return to you. ⁷Remain in the same house, eating and drinking what they offer, for the worker is worthy of his wages. Don't be moving from house to house. ⁸When you enter any town, and they welcome you, eat the things set before you. ⁹Heal the sick who are there, and tell them, 'The kingdom of God has come near you.' ¹⁰When you enter any town, and they don't welcome you, go out into its streets and say, ¹¹'We are wiping off as a witness against you even the dust of your

ᴬ9:39 Lit *convulsions with foam*   ᴮ9:39 Or *bruising, or mauling*   ᶜ9:41 Or *corrupt, or perverted, or twisted*; Dt 32:5   ᴰ9:44 Lit *Put these words in your ears*   ᴱ9:45 Lit *about this statement*   ᶠ9:48 Or *receives*, throughout the verse   ᴳ9:50 Other mss read *against us is for us*   ᴴ9:51 His ascension   ᴵ9:51 Lit *He stiffened His face to go*; Is 50:7   ᴶ9:54 Other mss add *as Elijah also did*   ᴷ9:55-56 Other mss add *and said, "You don't know what kind of spirit you belong to.* ⁵⁶ *For the Son of Man did not come to destroy people's lives but to save them,"*   ᴸ9:58 Wild birds, as opposed to domestic birds   ᴹ9:59 Not necessarily meaning his father was already dead   ᴺ10:1 Other mss read *72*   ᴼ10:6 A peaceful person; one open to the message of the kingdom town that clings to our feet. Know this for certain: The kingdom of God has come near.' ¹²I tell you, on that day it will be more tolerable for Sodom than for that town.

¹³"Woe to you, Chorazin! Woe to you, Bethsaida! For if the miracles that were done in you had been done in Tyre and Sidon, they would have repented long ago, sitting in sackcloth and ashes! ¹⁴But it will be more tolerable for Tyre and Sidon at the judgment than for you. ¹⁵And you, Capernaum, will you be exalted to heaven? No, you will go down to Hades! ¹⁶Whoever listens to you listens to Me. Whoever rejects you rejects Me. And whoever rejects Me rejects the One who sent Me."

¹⁷The Seventy^A returned with joy, saying, "Lord, even the demons submit to us in Your name."

¹⁸He said to them, "I watched Satan fall from heaven like a lightning flash. ¹⁹Look, I have given you the authority to trample on snakes and scorpions and over all the power of the enemy; nothing will ever harm you. ²⁰However, don't rejoice that^B the spirits submit to you, but rejoice that your names are written in heaven."

²¹In that same hour He^C rejoiced in the Holy^D Spirit and said, "I praise^E You, Father, Lord of heaven and earth, because You have hidden these things from the wise and the learned and have revealed them to infants. Yes, Father, because this was Your good pleasure.^F ²²All things have^G been entrusted to Me by My Father. No one knows who the Son is except the Father, and who the Father is except the Son, and anyone to whom the Son desires^H to reveal Him."

²³Then turning to His disciples He said privately, "The eyes that see the things you see are blessed! ²⁴For I tell you that many prophets and kings wanted to see the things you see yet didn't see them; to hear the things you hear yet didn't hear them."

²⁵Just then an expert in the law stood up to test Him, saying, "Teacher, what must I do to inherit eternal life?"

²⁶"What is written in the law?" He asked him. "How do you read it?"

²⁷He answered:

Love the Lord your God with all your heart, with all your soul, with all your strength, and with all your mind; and **your neighbor as yourself.**^I

²⁸"You've answered correctly," He told him. "Do this and you will live."

²⁹But wanting to justify himself, he asked Jesus, "And who is my neighbor?"

³⁰Jesus took up the question and said: "A man was going down from Jerusalem to Jericho and fell into the hands of robbers. They stripped him, beat him up, and fled, leaving him half dead. ³¹A priest happened to be going down that road. When he saw him, he passed by on the other side. ³²In the same way, a Levite, when he arrived at the place and saw him, passed by on the other side. ³³But a Samaritan on his journey came up to him, and when he saw the man, he had compassion. ³⁴He went over to him and bandaged his wounds, pouring on olive oil and wine. Then he put him on his own animal, brought him to an inn, and took care of him. ³⁵The next day^J he took out two denarii, gave them to the innkeeper, and said, 'Take care of him. When I come back I'll reimburse you for whatever extra you spend.'

³⁶"Which of these three do you think proved to be a neighbor to the man who fell into the hands of the robbers?"

³⁷"The one who showed mercy to him," he said.

Then Jesus told him, "Go and do the same."

³⁸While they were traveling, He entered a village, and a woman named Martha welcomed Him into her home.^K ³⁹She had a sister named Mary, who also sat at the Lord's^L feet and was listening to what He said.^M ⁴⁰But Martha was distracted by her many tasks, and she came up and asked, "Lord, don't You care that my sister has left me to serve alone? So tell her to give me a hand."^N

⁴¹The Lord^C answered her, "Martha, Martha, you are worried and upset about many things, ⁴²but one thing is necessary. Mary has made the right choice,^O and it will not be taken away from her."

^A10:17 Other mss read The Seventy-two ^B10:20 Lit don't rejoice in this, that ^C10:21,41 Other mss read Jesus ^D10:21 Other mss omit Holy ^E10:21 Or thank, or confess ^F10:21 Lit was well-pleasing in Your sight ^G10:22 Other mss read And turning to the disciples, He said, "Everything has ^H10:22 Or wills, or chooses ^I10:27 Lv 19:18; Dt 6:5 ^J10:35 Other mss add as he was leaving ^K10:38 Other mss omit into her home ^L10:39 Other mss read at Jesus' ^M10:39 Lit to His word or message ^N10:40 Or tell her to help me ^O10:42 Lit has chosen the good part

11 He was praying in a certain place, and when He finished, one of His disciples said to Him, "Lord, teach us to pray, just as John also taught his disciples."

² He said to them, "Whenever you pray, say:

Father,[A]
Your name be honored as holy.
Your kingdom come.[B]
³ Give us each day our daily bread.[C]
⁴ And forgive us our sins,
   for we ourselves also forgive everyone
   in debt to us.[D]
And do not bring us into temptation."[E]

⁵ He also said to them: "Suppose one of you[F] has a friend and goes to him at midnight and says to him, 'Friend, lend me three loaves of bread, ⁶ because a friend of mine on a journey has come to me, and I don't have anything to offer him.'[G] ⁷ Then he will answer from inside and say, 'Don't bother me! The door is already locked, and my children and I have gone to bed. I can't get up to give you anything.' ⁸ I tell you, even though he won't get up and give him anything because he is his friend, yet because of his friend's persistence,[H] he will get up and give him as much as he needs.

⁹ "So I say to you, keep asking,[I] and it will be given to you. Keep searching,[J] and you will find. Keep knocking,[K] and the door will be opened to you. ¹⁰ For everyone who asks receives, and the one who searches finds, and to the one who knocks, the door will be opened. ¹¹ What father among you, if his son[L] asks for a fish, will give him a snake instead of a fish? ¹² Or if he asks for an egg, will give him a scorpion? ¹³ If you then, who are evil, know how to give good gifts to your children, how much more will the heavenly Father give[M] the Holy Spirit to those who ask Him?"

¹⁴ Now He was driving out a demon that was mute.[N] When the demon came out, the man who had been mute, spoke, and the crowds were amazed. ¹⁵ But some of them said, "He drives out demons by Beelzebul, the ruler of the demons!" ¹⁶ And others, as a test, were demanding of Him a sign from heaven.

¹⁷ Knowing their thoughts, He told them: "Every kingdom divided against itself is headed for destruction, and a house divided against itself falls. ¹⁸ If Satan also is divided against himself, how will his kingdom stand? For you say I drive out demons by Beelzebul. ¹⁹ And if I drive out demons by Beelzebul, who is it your sons[O] drive them out by? For this reason they will be your judges. ²⁰ If I drive out demons by the finger of God, then the kingdom of God has come to you. ²¹ When a strong man, fully armed, guards his estate, his possessions are secure.[P] ²² But when one stronger than he attacks and overpowers him, he takes from him all his weapons[Q] he trusted in, and divides up his plunder. ²³ Anyone who is not with Me is against Me, and anyone who does not gather with Me scatters.

²⁴ "When an unclean spirit comes out of a man, it roams through waterless places looking for rest, and not finding rest, it then[R] says, 'I'll go back to my house where I came from.' ²⁵ And returning, it finds the house swept and put in order. ²⁶ Then it goes and brings seven other spirits more evil than itself, and they enter and settle down there. As a result, that man's last condition is worse than the first."

²⁷ As He was saying these things, a woman from the crowd raised her voice and said to Him, "The womb that bore You and the one who nursed You are blessed!"

²⁸ He said, "Even more, those who hear the word of God and keep it are blessed!"

²⁹ As the crowds were increasing, He began saying: "This generation is an evil generation. It demands a sign, but no sign will be given to it except the sign of Jonah.[S] ³⁰ For just as Jonah became a sign to the people of Nineveh, so also the Son of Man will be to this generation. ³¹ The queen of the south will rise up at the judgment with the men of this generation and condemn them, because she came from the ends of the earth to hear the wisdom of Solomon, and look—something greater than Solomon is here! ³² The men of Nineveh will rise up at the judgment with this generation and condemn it, because they repented at Jonah's proclamation, and look—something greater than Jonah is here!

³³ "No one lights a lamp and puts it in the cellar or under a basket,[T] but on a lampstand,

A11:2 Other mss read *Our Father in heaven*   B11:2 Other mss add *Your will be done on earth as it is in heaven*   C11:3 Or *our bread for tomorrow*   D11:4 Or *everyone who wrongs us*   E11:4 Other mss add *But deliver us from the evil one*   F11:5 Lit *Who of you*   G11:6 Lit *I have nothing to set before him*   H11:8 Or *annoying persistence, or shamelessness*   I11:9 Or *you, ask*   J11:9 Or *Search*   K11:9 Or *Knock*   L11:11 Other mss read *son asks for bread, would give him a stone? Or if he*   M11:13 Lit *the Father from heaven will give*   N11:14 A demon that caused the man to be mute   O11:19 Your exorcists   P11:21 Lit *his possessions are in peace*   Q11:22 Gk *panoplia*, the armor and weapons of a foot soldier; Eph 6:11,13   R11:24 Other mss omit *then*   S11:29 Other mss add *the prophet*   T11:33 Other mss omit *or under a basket* so that those who come in may see its light. [34]Your eye is the lamp of the body. When your eye is good, your whole body is also full of light. But when it is bad, your body is also full of darkness. [35]Take care then, that the light in you is not darkness. [36]If, therefore, your whole body is full of light, with no part of it in darkness, it will be entirely illuminated, as when a lamp shines its light on you."[A]

[37]As He was speaking, a Pharisee asked Him to dine with him. So He went in and reclined at the table. [38]When the Pharisee saw this, he was amazed that He did not first perform the ritual washing[B] before dinner. [39]But the Lord said to him: "Now you Pharisees clean the outside of the cup and dish, but inside you are full of greed and evil. [40]Fools! Didn't He who made the outside make the inside too? [41]But give from what is within to the poor,[C] and then everything is clean for you.

[42]"But woe to you Pharisees! You give a tenth[D] of mint, rue, and every kind of herb, and you bypass[E] justice and love for God.[F] These things you should have done without neglecting the others.

[43]"Woe to you Pharisees! You love the front seat in the synagogues and greetings in the marketplaces.

[44]"Woe to you![G] You are like unmarked graves; the people who walk over them don't know it."

[45]One of the experts in the law answered Him, "Teacher, when You say these things You insult us too."

[46]Then He said: "Woe also to you experts in the law! You load people with burdens that are hard to carry, yet you yourselves don't touch these burdens with one of your fingers.

[47]"Woe to you! You build monuments[H] to the prophets, and your fathers killed them. [48]Therefore, you are witnesses that you approve[I] the deeds of your fathers, for they killed them, and you build their monuments.[J] [49]Because of this, the wisdom of God said, 'I will send them prophets and apostles, and some of them they will kill and persecute,' [50]so that this generation may be held responsible for the blood of all the prophets shed since the foundation of the world[K]— [51]from the blood of Abel to the blood of Zechariah, who perished between the altar and the sanctuary.

"Yes, I tell you, this generation will be held responsible.[L]

[52]"Woe to you experts in the law! You have taken away the key of knowledge! You didn't go in yourselves, and you hindered those who were going in."

[53]When He left there,[M] the scribes and the Pharisees began to oppose Him fiercely and to cross-examine Him about many things; [54]they were lying in wait for Him to trap Him in something He said.[N]

12 In these circumstances,[O] a crowd of many thousands came together, so that they were trampling on one another. He began to say to His disciples first: "Be on your guard against the yeast[P] of the Pharisees, which is hypocrisy. [2]There is nothing covered that won't be uncovered, nothing hidden that won't be made known. [3]Therefore, whatever you have said in the dark will be heard in the light, and what you have whispered in an ear in private rooms will be proclaimed on the housetops.

[4]"And I say to you, My friends, don't fear those who kill the body, and after that can do nothing more. [5]But I will show you the One to fear: Fear Him who has authority to throw people into hell after death. Yes, I say to you, this is the One to fear! [6]Aren't five sparrows sold for two pennies?[Q] Yet not one of them is forgotten in God's sight. [7]Indeed, the hairs of your head are all counted. Don't be afraid; you are worth more than many sparrows!

[8]"And I say to you, anyone who acknowledges Me before men, the Son of Man will also acknowledge him before the angels of God, [9]but whoever denies Me before men will be denied before the angels of God. [10]Anyone who speaks a word against the Son of Man will be forgiven, but the one who blasphemes against the Holy Spirit will not be forgiven. [11]Whenever they bring you before synagogues and rulers and authorities, don't worry about how you should defend yourselves or what you should say. [12]For the Holy Spirit will teach you at that very hour what must be said."

[A]11:36 Or shines on you with its rays   [B]11:38 Lit He did not first wash   [C]11:41 Or But donate from the heart as charity   [D]11:42 Or a tithe   [E]11:42 Or neglect   [F]11:42 Lit the justice and the love of God   [G]11:44 Other mss read you scribes and Pharisees, hypocrites!   [H]11:47 Or graves   [I]11:48 Lit witnesses and approve   [J]11:48 Other mss omit their monuments   [K]11:50 Lit so that the blood of all ... world may be required of this generation,   [L]11:51 Lit you, it will be required of this generation   [M]11:53 Other mss read And as He was saying these things to them   [N]11:54 Other mss add so that they might bring charges against Him   [O]12:1 Or Meanwhile, or At this time, or During this period   [P]12:1 Or leaven   [Q]12:6 Lit two assaria; the assarion (sg) was a small copper coin

¹³Someone from the crowd said to Him, "Teacher, tell my brother to divide the inheritance with me."

¹⁴"Friend,"ᴬ He said to him, "who appointed Me a judge or arbitrator over you?" ¹⁵He then told them, "Watch out and be on guard against all greed because one's life is not in the abundance of his possessions."

¹⁶Then He told them a parable: "A rich man's land was very productive. ¹⁷He thought to himself, 'What should I do, since I don't have anywhere to store my crops? ¹⁸I will do this,' he said. 'I'll tear down my barns and build bigger ones and store all my grain and my goods there. ¹⁹Then I'll say to myself, "Youᴮ have many goods stored up for many years. Take it easy; eat, drink, and enjoy yourself."'

²⁰"But God said to him, 'You fool! This very night your life is demanded of you. And the things you have prepared—whose will they be?'

²¹"That's how it is with the one who stores up treasure for himself and is not rich toward God."

²²Then He said to His disciples: "Therefore I tell you, don't worry about your life, what you will eat; or about the body, what you will wear. ²³For life is more than food and the body more than clothing. ²⁴Consider the ravens: They don't sow or reap; they don't have a storeroom or a barn; yet God feeds them. Aren't you worth much more than the birds? ²⁵Can any of you add a cubit to his heightᶜ by worrying? ²⁶If then you're not able to do even a little thing, why worry about the rest?

²⁷"Consider how the wildflowers grow: They don't labor or spin thread. Yet I tell you, not even Solomon in all his splendor was adorned like one of these! ²⁸If that's how God clothes the grass, which is in the field today and is thrown into the furnace tomorrow, how much more will He do for you—you of little faith? ²⁹Don't keep striving for what you should eat and what you should drink, and don't be anxious. ³⁰For the Gentile world eagerly seeks all these things, and your Father knows that you need them.

³¹"But seek His kingdom, and these things will be provided for you. ³²Don't be afraid, little flock, because your Father delights to give you the kingdom. ³³Sell your possessions and give to the poor. Make money-bags for yourselves that won't grow old, an inexhaustible treasure in heaven, where no thief comes near and no moth destroys. ³⁴For where your treasure is, there your heart will be also.

³⁵"Be ready for serviceᴰ and have your lamps lit. ³⁶You must be like people waiting for their master to returnᴱ from the wedding banquet so that when he comes and knocks, they can open the door for him at once. ³⁷Those slaves the master will find alert when he comes will be blessed. I assure you: He will get ready,ᶠ have them recline at the table, then come and serve them. ³⁸If he comes in the middle of the night, or even near dawn,ᴳ and finds them alert, those slaves are blessed. ³⁹But know this: If the homeowner had known at what hour the thief was coming, he would not have let his house be broken into. ⁴⁰You also be ready, because the Son of Man is coming at an hour that you do not expect."

⁴¹"Lord," Peter asked, "are You telling this parable to us or to everyone?"

⁴²The Lord said: "Who then is the faithful and sensible manager his master will put in charge of his household servants to give them their allotted food at the proper time? ⁴³That slave whose master finds him working when he comes will be rewarded. ⁴⁴I tell you the truth: He will put him in charge of all his possessions. ⁴⁵But if that slave says in his heart, 'My master is delaying his coming,' and starts to beat the male and female slaves, and to eat and drink and get drunk, ⁴⁶that slave's master will come on a day he does not expect him and at an hour he does not know. He will cut him to piecesᴴ and assign him a place with the unbelievers.ᴵ ⁴⁷And that slave who knew his master's will and didn't prepare himself or do itᴶ will be severely beaten. ⁴⁸But the one who did not know and did things deserving of blows will be beaten lightly. Much will be required of everyone who has been given much. And even more will be expected of the one who has been entrusted with more.ᴷ

⁴⁹"I came to bring fire on the earth, and how I wish it were already set ablaze! ⁵⁰But I have a baptism to be baptized with, and how it consumes Me until it is finished! ⁵¹Do you think

---

ᴬ12:14 Lit Man   ᴮ12:19 Lit say to my soul, "Soul, you   ᶜ12:25 Or add one moment to his life-span   ᴰ12:35 Lit Let your loins be girded; an idiom for tying up loose outer clothing in preparation for action; Ex 12:11   ᴱ12:36 Lit master, when he should return   ᶠ12:37 Lit will gird himself   ᴳ12:38 Lit even in the second or third watch   ᴴ12:46 Lit him in two   ᴵ12:46 Or unfaithful, or untrustworthy   ᴶ12:47 Lit or do toward his will   ᴷ12:48 Or much

that I came here to give peace to the earth? No, I tell you, but rather division! ⁵²From now on, five in one household will be divided: three against two, and two against three.

⁵³   They will be divided, father against son,
            son against father,
        mother against daughter,
            daughter against mother,
        mother-in-law against
            her daughter-in-law,
        and daughter-in-law
            against mother-in-law."ᴬ

⁵⁴He also said to the crowds: "When you see a cloud rising in the west, right away you say, 'A storm is coming,' and so it does. ⁵⁵And when the south wind is blowing, you say, 'It's going to be a scorcher!' and it is. ⁵⁶Hypocrites! You know how to interpret the appearance of the earth and the sky, but why don't you know how to interpret this time?

⁵⁷"Why don't you judge for yourselves what is right? ⁵⁸As you are going with your adversary to the ruler, make an effort to settle with him on the way. Then he won't drag you before the judge, the judge hand you over to the bailiff, and the bailiff throw you into prison. ⁵⁹I tell you, you will never get out of there until you have paid the last cent."ᴮ

13 At that time, some people came and reported to Him about the Galileans whose blood Pilate had mixed with their sacrifices. ²And Heᶜ responded to them, "Do you think that these Galileans were more sinful than all Galileans because they suffered these things? ³No, I tell you; but unless you repent, you will all perish as well! ⁴Or those 18 that the tower in Siloam fell on and killed—do you think they were more sinful than all the people who live in Jerusalem? ⁵No, I tell you; but unless you repent, you will all perish as well!"

⁶And He told this parable: "A man had a fig tree that was planted in his vineyard. He came looking for fruit on it and found none. ⁷He told the vineyard worker, 'Listen, for three years I have come looking for fruit on this fig tree and haven't found any. Cut it down! Why should it even waste the soil?'

⁸"But he replied to him, 'Sir,ᴰ leave it this year also, until I dig around it and fertilize it.

⁹Perhaps it will bear fruit next year, but if not, you can cut it down.'"

¹⁰As He was teaching in one of the synagogues on the Sabbath, ¹¹a woman was there who had been disabled by a spiritᴱ for over 18 years. She was bent over and could not straighten up at all.ᶠ ¹²When Jesus saw her, He called out to her,ᴳ "Woman, you are free of your disability." ¹³Then He laid His hands on her, and instantly she was restored and began to glorify God.

¹⁴But the leader of the synagogue, indignant because Jesus had healed on the Sabbath, responded by telling the crowd, "There are six days when work should be done; therefore come on those days and be healed and not on the Sabbath day."

¹⁵But the Lord answered him and said, "Hypocrites! Doesn't each one of you untie his ox or donkey from the feeding trough on the Sabbath and lead it to water? ¹⁶Satan has bound this woman, a daughter of Abraham, for 18 years—shouldn't she be untied from this bondage on the Sabbath day?"

¹⁷When He had said these things, all His adversaries were humiliated, but the whole crowd was rejoicing over all the glorious things He was doing.

¹⁸He said, therefore, "What is the kingdom of God like, and what can I compare it to? ¹⁹It's like a mustard seed that a man took and sowed in his garden. It grew and became a tree, and the birds of the sky nested in its branches."

²⁰Again He said, "What can I compare the kingdom of God to? ²¹It's like yeast that a woman took and mixed into 50 poundsᴴ of flour until it spread through the entire mixture."ᴵ

²²He went through one town and village after another, teaching and making His way to Jerusalem. ²³"Lord," someone asked Him, "are there few being saved?"ᴶ

He said to them, ²⁴"Make every effort to enter through the narrow door, because I tell you, many will try to enter and won't be able ²⁵once the homeowner gets up and shuts the door. Then you will standᴷ outside and knock on the door, saying, 'Lord, open up for us!' He will answer you, 'I don't know you or where you're from.' ²⁶Then you will say,ᴸ 'We ate and drank in Your presence, and You taught

ᴬ12:53 Mc 7:6   ᴮ12:59 Gk lepton, the smallest and least valuable copper coin in use   ᶜ13:2 Other mss read Jesus   ᴰ13:8 Or Lord   ᴱ13:11 Lit had a spirit of disability   ᶠ13:11 Or straighten up completely   ᴳ13:12 Or He summoned her   ᴴ13:21 Lit 3 sata; about 40 quarts   ᴵ13:21 Or until all of it was leavened   ᴶ13:23 Or are the saved few? (in number); lit are those being saved few?   ᴷ13:25 Lit you will begin to stand   ᴸ13:26 Lit you will begin to say in our streets!' ²⁷But He will say, 'I tell you, I don't know you or where you're from. Get away from Me, all you workers of unrighteousness!' ²⁸There will be weeping and gnashing of teeth in that place, when you see Abraham, Isaac, Jacob, and all the prophets in the kingdom of God, but yourselves thrown out. ²⁹They will come from east and west, from north and south, and recline at the table in the kingdom of God. ³⁰Note this: Some are last who will be first, and some are first who will be last."

³¹At that time some Pharisees came and told Him, "Go, get out of here! Herod wants to kill You!"

³²He said to them, "Go tell that fox, 'Look! I'm driving out demons and performing healings today and tomorrow, and on the third day[A] I will complete My work.'[B] ³³Yet I must travel today, tomorrow, and the next day, because it is not possible for a prophet to perish outside of Jerusalem!

³⁴"Jerusalem, Jerusalem! She who kills the prophets and stones those who are sent to her. How often I wanted to gather your children together, as a hen gathers her chicks under her wings, but you were not willing! ³⁵See, your house[C] is abandoned to you. And I tell you, you will not see Me until the time comes when you say, **'He who comes in the name of the Lord is the blessed One'!"[D]**

14 One Sabbath, when He went to eat[E] at the house of one of the leading Pharisees, they were watching Him closely. ²There in front of Him was a man whose body was swollen with fluid.[F] ³In response, Jesus asked the law experts and the Pharisees, "Is it lawful to heal on the Sabbath or not?" ⁴But they kept silent. He took the man, healed him, and sent him away. ⁵And to them, He said, "Which of you whose son or ox falls into a well, will not immediately pull him out on the Sabbath day?" ⁶To this they could find no answer.

⁷He told a parable to those who were invited, when He noticed how they would choose the best places for themselves: ⁸"When you are invited by someone to a wedding banquet, don't recline at the best place, because a more distinguished person than you may have been invited by your host.[G] ⁹The one who invited both of you may come and say to you, 'Give

your place to this man,' and then in humiliation, you will proceed to take the lowest place. ¹⁰"But when you are invited, go and recline in the lowest place, so that when the one who invited you comes, he will say to you, 'Friend, move up higher.' You will then be honored in the presence of all the other guests. ¹¹For everyone who exalts himself will be humbled, and the one who humbles himself will be exalted."

¹²He also said to the one who had invited Him, "When you give a lunch or a dinner, don't invite your friends, your brothers, your relatives, or your rich neighbors, because they might invite you back, and you would be repaid. ¹³On the contrary, when you host a banquet, invite those who are poor, maimed, lame, or blind. ¹⁴And you will be blessed, because they cannot repay you; for you will be repaid at the resurrection of the righteous."

¹⁵When one of those who reclined at the table with Him heard these things, he said to Him, "The one who will eat bread in the kingdom of God is blessed!"

¹⁶Then He told him: "A man was giving a large banquet and invited many. ¹⁷At the time of the banquet, he sent his slave to tell those who were invited, 'Come, because everything is now ready.'

¹⁸"But without exception[H] they all began to make excuses. The first one said to him, 'I have bought a field, and I must go out and see it. I ask you to excuse me.'

¹⁹"Another said, 'I have bought five yoke of oxen, and I'm going to try them out. I ask you to excuse me.'

²⁰"And another said, 'I just got married,[I] and therefore I'm unable to come.'

²¹"So the slave came back and reported these things to his master. Then in anger, the master of the house told his slave, 'Go out quickly into the streets and alleys of the city, and bring in here the poor, maimed, blind, and lame!'

²²"'Master,' the slave said, 'what you ordered has been done, and there's still room.'

²³"Then the master told the slave, 'Go out into the highways and lanes and make them come in, so that my house may be filled. ²⁴For I tell you, not one of those men who were invited will enjoy my banquet!'"

[25] Now great crowds were traveling with Him. So He turned and said to them: [26] "If anyone comes to Me and does not hate his own father and mother, wife and children, brothers and sisters—yes, and even his own life—he cannot be My disciple. [27] Whoever does not bear his own cross and come after Me cannot be My disciple.

[28] "For which of you, wanting to build a tower, doesn't first sit down and calculate the cost to see if he has enough to complete it? [29] Otherwise, after he has laid the foundation and cannot finish it, all the onlookers will begin to make fun of him, [30] saying, 'This man started to build and wasn't able to finish.'

[31] "Or what king, going to war against another king, will not first sit down and decide if he is able with 10,000 to oppose the one who comes against him with 20,000? [32] If not, while the other is still far off, he sends a delegation and asks for terms of peace. [33] In the same way, therefore, every one of you who does not say good-bye to[A] all his possessions cannot be My disciple.

[34] "Now, salt is good, but if salt should lose its taste, how will it be made salty? [35] It isn't fit for the soil or for the manure pile; they throw it out. Anyone who has ears to hear should listen!"

15 All the tax collectors and sinners were approaching to listen to Him. [2] And the Pharisees and scribes were complaining, "This man welcomes sinners and eats with them!"

[3] So He told them this parable: [4] "What man among you, who has 100 sheep and loses one of them, does not leave the 99 in the open field[B] and go after the lost one until he finds it? [5] When he has found it, he joyfully puts it on his shoulders, [6] and coming home, he calls his friends and neighbors together, saying to them, 'Rejoice with me, because I have found my lost sheep!' [7] I tell you, in the same way, there will be more joy in heaven over one sinner who repents than over 99 righteous people who don't need repentance.

[8] "Or what woman who has 10 silver coins,[C] if she loses one coin, does not light a lamp, sweep the house, and search carefully until she finds it? [9] When she finds it, she calls her women friends and neighbors together, saying, 'Rejoice with me, because I have found

the silver coin I lost!' [10] I tell you, in the same way, there is joy in the presence of God's angels over one sinner who repents."

[11] He also said: "A man had two sons. [12] The younger of them said to his father, 'Father, give me the share of the estate I have coming to me.' So he distributed the assets[D] to them. [13] Not many days later, the younger son gathered together all he had and traveled to a distant country, where he squandered his estate in foolish living. [14] After he had spent everything, a severe famine struck that country, and he had nothing.[E] [15] Then he went to work for[F] one of the citizens of that country, who sent him into his fields to feed pigs. [16] He longed to eat his fill from[G] the carob pods[H] the pigs were eating, but no one would give him any. [17] When he came to his senses,[I] he said, 'How many of my father's hired hands have more than enough food, and here I am dying of hunger![J] [18] I'll get up, go to my father, and say to him, Father, I have sinned against heaven and in your sight. [19] I'm no longer worthy to be called your son. Make me like one of your hired hands.' [20] So he got up and went to his father. But while the son was still a long way off, his father saw him and was filled with compassion. He ran, threw his arms around his neck,[K] and kissed him. [21] The son said to him, 'Father, I have sinned against heaven and in your sight. I'm no longer worthy to be called your son.'

[22] "But the father told his slaves, 'Quick! Bring out the best robe and put it on him; put a ring on his finger[L] and sandals on his feet. [23] Then bring the fattened calf and slaughter it, and let's celebrate with a feast, [24] because this son of mine was dead and is alive again; he was lost and is found!' So they began to celebrate.

[25] "Now his older son was in the field; as he came near the house, he heard music and dancing. [26] So he summoned one of the servants and asked what these things meant. [27] 'Your brother is here,' he told him, 'and your father has slaughtered the fattened calf because he has him back safe and sound.'[M] [28] "Then he became angry and didn't want to go in. So his father came out and pleaded with him. [29] But he replied to his father, 'Look, I have been slaving many years for you, and

I have never disobeyed your orders, yet you never gave me a young goat so I could celebrate with my friends. [30]But when this son of yours came, who has devoured your assets[A] with prostitutes, you slaughtered the fattened calf for him.'

[31]"'Son,'[B] he said to him, 'you are always with me, and everything I have is yours. [32]But we had to celebrate and rejoice, because this brother of yours was dead and is alive again; he was lost and is found.'"

16 He also said to the disciples: "There was a rich man who received an accusation that his manager was squandering his possessions. [2]So he called the manager in and asked, 'What is this I hear about you? Give an account of your management, because you can no longer be my manager.'

[3]"Then the manager said to himself, 'What should I do, since my master is taking the management away from me? I'm not strong enough to dig; I'm ashamed to beg. [4]I know what I'll do so that when I'm removed from management, people will welcome me into their homes.'

[5]"So he summoned each one of his master's debtors. 'How much do you owe my master?' he asked the first one.

[6]"'A hundred measures of olive oil,' he said.

"'Take your invoice,' he told him, 'sit down quickly, and write 50.'

[7]"Next he asked another, 'How much do you owe?'

"'A hundred measures of wheat,' he said.

"'Take your invoice,' he told him, 'and write 80.'

[8]"The master praised the unrighteous manager because he had acted astutely. For the sons of this age are more astute than the sons of light in dealing with their own people.[C] [9]And I tell you, make friends for yourselves by means of the unrighteous money so that when it fails,[D] they may welcome you into eternal dwellings. [10]Whoever is faithful in very little is also faithful in much, and whoever is unrighteous in very little is also unrighteous in much. [11]So if you have not been faithful with the unrighteous money, who will trust you with what is genuine? [12]And if you have not been faithful with what belongs to someone else, who will give you what is your own? [13]No household

slave can be the slave of two masters, since either he will hate one and love the other, or he will be devoted to one and despise the other. You can't be slaves to both God and money."

[14]The Pharisees, who were lovers of money, were listening to all these things and scoffing at Him. [15]And He told them: "You are the ones who justify yourselves in the sight of others, but God knows your hearts. For what is highly admired by people is revolting in God's sight.

[16]"The Law and the Prophets were[E] until John; since then, the good news of the kingdom of God has been proclaimed, and everyone is strongly urged to enter it.[F] [17]But it is easier for heaven and earth to pass away than for one stroke of a letter in the law to drop out.

[18]"Everyone who divorces his wife and marries another woman commits adultery, and everyone who marries a woman divorced from her husband commits adultery.

[19]"There was a rich man who would dress in purple and fine linen, feasting lavishly every day. [20]But a poor man named Lazarus, covered with sores, was left at his gate. [21]He longed to be filled with what fell from the rich man's table, but instead the dogs would come and lick his sores. [22]One day the poor man died and was carried away by the angels to Abraham's side.[G] The rich man also died and was buried. [23]And being in torment in Hades, he looked up and saw Abraham a long way off, with Lazarus at his side. [24]'Father Abraham!' he called out, 'Have mercy on me and send Lazarus to dip the tip of his finger in water and cool my tongue, because I am in agony in this flame!'

[25]"'Son,'[H] Abraham said, 'remember that during your life you received your good things, just as Lazarus received bad things, but now he is comforted here, while you are in agony. [26]Besides all this, a great chasm has been fixed between us and you, so that those who want to pass over from here to you cannot; neither can those from there cross over to us.'

[27]"'Father,' he said, 'then I beg you to send him to my father's house— [28]because I have five brothers—to warn them, so they won't also come to this place of torment.'

[29]"But Abraham said, 'They have Moses and the prophets; they should listen to them.'

A15:30 Lit livelihood, or living   B15:31 Or Child   C16:8 Lit own generation   D16:9 Other mss read when you fail or pass away   E16:16 Perhaps were proclaimed, or were in effect   F16:16 Or everyone is forcing his way into it   G16:22 Or to Abraham's bosom; lit to the fold of Abraham's robe; Jn 13:23   H16:25 Lit Child

³⁰"'No, father Abraham,' he said. 'But if someone from the dead goes to them, they will repent.'

³¹"But he told him, 'If they don't listen to Moses and the prophets, they will not be persuaded if someone rises from the dead.'"

17 He said to His disciples, "Offenses^A will certainly come,^B but woe to the one they come through! ²It would be better for him if a millstone^C were hung around his neck and he were thrown into the sea than for him to cause one of these little ones to stumble. ³Be on your guard. If your brother sins,^D rebuke him, and if he repents, forgive him. ⁴And if he sins against you seven times in a day, and comes back to you seven times, saying, 'I repent,' you must forgive him."

⁵The apostles said to the Lord, "Increase our faith."

⁶"If you have faith the size of^E a mustard seed," the Lord said, "you can say to this mulberry tree, 'Be uprooted and planted in the sea,' and it will obey you.

⁷"Which one of you having a slave tending sheep or plowing will say to him when he comes in from the field, 'Come at once and sit down to eat'? ⁸Instead, will he not tell him, 'Prepare something for me to eat, get ready,^F and serve me while I eat and drink; later you can eat and drink'? ⁹Does he thank that slave because he did what was commanded?^G ¹⁰In the same way, when you have done all that you were commanded, you should say, 'We are good-for-nothing slaves; we've only done our duty.'"

¹¹While traveling to Jerusalem, He passed between^H Samaria and Galilee. ¹²As He entered a village, 10 men with serious skin diseases met Him. They stood at a distance ¹³and raised their voices, saying, "Jesus, Master, have mercy on us!"

¹⁴When He saw them, He told them, "Go and show yourselves to the priests." And while they were going, they were healed.^I

¹⁵But one of them, seeing that he was healed, returned and, with a loud voice, gave glory to God. ¹⁶He fell facedown at His feet, thanking Him. And he was a Samaritan.

¹⁷Then Jesus said, "Were not 10 cleansed? Where are the nine? ¹⁸Didn't any return^J to

give glory to God except this foreigner?" ¹⁹And He told him, "Get up and go on your way. Your faith has made you well."^K

²⁰Being asked by the Pharisees when the kingdom of God will come, He answered them, "The kingdom of God is not coming with something observable; ²¹no one will say,^L 'Look here!' or 'There!' For you see, the kingdom of God is among you."

²²Then He told the disciples: "The days are coming when you will long to see one of the days of the Son of Man, but you won't see it. ²³They will say to you, 'Look there!' or 'Look here!' Don't follow or run after them. ²⁴For as the lightning flashes from horizon to horizon and lights up the sky, so the Son of Man will be in His day. ²⁵But first He must suffer many things and be rejected by this generation.

²⁶"Just as it was in the days of Noah, so it will be in the days of the Son of Man: ²⁷People went on eating, drinking, marrying and giving in marriage until the day Noah boarded the ark, and the flood came and destroyed them all. ²⁸It will be the same as it was in the days of Lot: People went on eating, drinking, buying, selling, planting, building. ²⁹But on the day Lot left Sodom, fire and sulfur rained from heaven and destroyed them all. ³⁰It will be like that on the day the Son of Man is revealed. ³¹On that day, a man on the housetop, whose belongings are in the house, must not come down to get them. Likewise the man who is in the field must not turn back. ³²Remember Lot's wife! ³³Whoever tries to make his life secure^M,N will lose it, and whoever loses his life will preserve it. ³⁴I tell you, on that night two will be in one bed: One will be taken and the other will be left. ³⁵Two women will be grinding grain together: One will be taken and the other left. [³⁶Two will be in a field: One will be taken, and the other will be left.]"^O

³⁷"Where, Lord?" they asked Him.

He said to them, "Where the corpse is, there also the vultures will be gathered."

18 He then told them a parable on the need for them to pray always and not become discouraged: ²"There was a judge in a certain town who didn't fear God or respect man. ³And a widow in that town kept coming to him, saying, 'Give me justice against my adversary.'

^A17:1 Or *Traps*, or *Bait-sticks*, or *Causes of stumbling*, or *Causes of sin*   ^B17:1 Lit *It is impossible for offenses not to come*   ^C17:2 Large stone used for grinding grains into flour   ^D17:3 Other mss add *against you*   ^E17:6 Lit *faith like*   ^F17:8 Or *eat, gird yourself*; lit *eat, tuck in your robe*   ^G17:9 Other mss add *I don't think so*   ^H17:11 Or *through the middle of*   ^I17:14 Lit *cleansed*   ^J17:18 Lit *Were they not found returning*   ^K17:19 Or *faith has saved you*   ^L17:21 Lit *they will not say*   ^M17:33 Other mss read *to save his life*   ^N17:33 Or *tries to retain his life*   ^O17:36 Other mss omit bracketed text

⁴"For a while he was unwilling, but later he said to himself, 'Even though I don't fear God or respect man, ⁵yet because this widow keeps pestering me,ᴬ I will give her justice, so she doesn't wear me outᴮ by her persistent coming.'"

⁶Then the Lord said, "Listen to what the unjust judge says. ⁷Will not God grant justice to His elect who cry out to Him day and night? Will He delay to help them?ᶜ ⁸I tell you that He will swiftly grant them justice. Nevertheless, when the Son of Man comes, will He find that faithᴰ on earth?"

⁹He also told this parable to some who trusted in themselves that they were righteous and looked down on everyone else: ¹⁰"Two men went up to the temple complex to pray, one a Pharisee and the other a tax collector. ¹¹The Pharisee took his standᴱ and was praying like this: 'God, I thank You that I'm not like other peopleᶠ—greedy, unrighteous, adulterers, or even like this tax collector. ¹²I fast twice a week; I give a tenthᴳ of everything I get.'

¹³"But the tax collector, standing far off, would not even raise his eyes to heaven but kept striking his chestᴴ and saying, 'God, turn Your wrath from me¹—a sinner!' ¹⁴I tell you, this one went down to his house justified rather than the other; because everyone who exalts himself will be humbled, but the one who humbles himself will be exalted."

¹⁵Some people were even bringing infants to Him so He might touch them, but when the disciples saw it, they rebuked them. ¹⁶Jesus, however, invited them: "Let the little children come to Me, and don't stop them, because the kingdom of God belongs to such as these. ¹⁷I assure you: Whoever does not welcome the kingdom of God like a little child will never enter it."

¹⁸A ruler asked Him, "Good Teacher, what must I do to inherit eternal life?"

¹⁹"Why do you call Me good?" Jesus asked him. "No one is good but One—God. ²⁰You know the commandments:

> Do not commit adultery;
> do not murder;
> do not steal;
> do not bear false witness;
> honor your father and mother."ᴶ

²¹"I have kept all these from my youth," he said.

²²When Jesus heard this, He told him, "You still lack one thing: Sell all that you have and distribute it to the poor, and you will have treasure in heaven. Then come, follow Me."

²³After he heard this, he became extremely sad, because he was very rich.

²⁴Seeing that he became sad,ᴷ Jesus said, "How hard it is for those who have wealth to enter the kingdom of God! ²⁵For it is easier for a camel to go through the eye of a needle than for a rich person to enter the kingdom of God."

²⁶Those who heard this asked, "Then who can be saved?"

²⁷He replied, "What is impossible with men is possible with God."

²⁸Then Peter said, "Look, we have left what we had and followed You."

²⁹So He said to them, "I assure you: There is no one who has left a house, wife or brothers, parents or children because of the kingdom of God, ³⁰who will not receive many times more at this time, and eternal life in the age to come."

³¹Then He took the Twelve aside and told them, "Listen! We are going up to Jerusalem. Everything that is written through the prophets about the Son of Man will be accomplished. ³²For He will be handed over to the Gentiles, and He will be mocked, insulted, spit on; ³³and after they flog Him, they will kill Him, and He will rise on the third day."

³⁴They understood none of these things. This sayingᴸ was hidden from them, and they did not grasp what was said.

³⁵As He drew near Jericho, a blind man was sitting by the road begging. ³⁶Hearing a crowd passing by, he inquired what this meant. ³⁷"Jesus the Nazarene is passing by," they told him.

³⁸So he called out, "Jesus, Son of David, have mercy on me!" ³⁹Then those in front told him to keep quiet,ᴹ but he kept crying out all the more, "Son of David, have mercy on me!"

⁴⁰Jesus stopped and commanded that he be brought to Him. When he drew near, He asked him, ⁴¹"What do you want Me to do for you?"

"Lord," he said, "I want to see!"

⁴²"Receive your sight!" Jesus told him. "Your faith has healed you."ᴺ ⁴³Instantly he could

ᴬ18:5 Lit *widow causes me trouble*   ᴮ18:5 Or *doesn't give me a black eye*, or *doesn't ruin my reputation*   ᶜ18:7 Or *Will He put up with them?*   ᴰ18:8 Or *faith*, or *that kind of faith*, or *any faith*, or *the faith*, or *faithfulness*; the faith that persists in prayer for God's vindication   ᴱ18:11 Or *Pharisee stood by himself*   ᶠ18:11 Or *like the rest of men*   ᴳ18:12 Or *give tithes*   ᴴ18:13 = mourning   ¹18:13 Lit *God, be propitious to me*; = May Your wrath be turned aside by the sacrifice   ᴶ18:20 Ex 20:12-16; Dt 5:16-20   ᴷ18:24 Other mss omit *he became sad*   ᴸ18:34 The meaning of the saying   ᴹ18:39 Or *those in front rebuked him*   ᴺ18:42 Or *has saved you* see, and he began to follow Him, glorifying God. All the people, when they saw it, gave praise to God.

19 He entered Jericho and was passing through. ²There was a man named Zacchaeus who was a chief tax collector, and he was rich. ³He was trying to see who Jesus was, but he was not able because of the crowd, since he was a short man. ⁴So running ahead, he climbed up a sycamore tree to see Jesus, since He was about to pass that way. ⁵When Jesus came to the place, He looked up and said to him, "Zacchaeus, hurry and come down because today I must stay at your house."

⁶So he quickly came down and welcomed Him joyfully. ⁷All who saw it began to complain, "He's gone to lodge with a sinful man!"

⁸But Zacchaeus stood there and said to the Lord, "Look, I'll giveᴬ half of my possessions to the poor, Lord! And if I have extorted anything from anyone, I'll payᴮ back four times as much!"

⁹"Today salvation has come to this house," Jesus told him, "because he too is a son of Abraham. ¹⁰For the Son of Man has come to seek and to save the lost."ᶜ

¹¹As they were listening to this, He went on to tell a parable because He was near Jerusalem, and they thought the kingdom of God was going to appear right away.

¹²Therefore He said: "A nobleman traveled to a far country to receive for himself authority to be kingᴰ and then return. ¹³He called 10 of his slaves, gave them 10 minas,ᴱ and told them, 'Engage in business until I come back.'

¹⁴"But his subjects hated him and sent a delegation after him, saying, 'We don't want this man to rule over us!'

¹⁵"At his return, having received the authority to be king,ᶠ he summoned those slaves he had given the money to, so he could find out how much they had made in business. ¹⁶The first came forward and said, 'Master, your mina has earned 10 more minas.'

¹⁷"'Well done, goodᴳ slave!' he told him. 'Because you have been faithful in a very small matter, have authority over 10 towns.'

¹⁸"The second came and said, 'Master, your mina has made five minas.'

¹⁹"So he said to him, 'You will be over five towns.'

²⁰"And another came and said, 'Master, here is your mina. I have kept it hidden away in a cloth ²¹because I was afraid of you, for you're a tough man: you collect what you didn't deposit and reap what you didn't sow.'

²²"He told him, 'I will judge you by what you have said,ᴴ you evil slave! If you knew I was a tough man, collecting what I didn't deposit and reaping what I didn't sow, ²³why didn't you put my money in the bank? And when I returned, I would have collected it with interest!' ²⁴So he said to those standing there, 'Take the mina away from him and give it to the one who has 10 minas.'

²⁵"But they said to him, 'Master, he has 10 minas.'

²⁶"'I tell you, that to everyone who has, more will be given; and from the one who does not have, even what he does have will be taken away. ²⁷But bring here these enemies of mine, who did not want me to rule over them, and slaughterᴵ them in my presence.'"

²⁸When He had said these things, He went on ahead, going up to Jerusalem. ²⁹As He approached Bethphage and Bethany, at the place called the Mount of Olives, He sent two of the disciples ³⁰and said, "Go into the village ahead of you. As you enter it, you will find a young donkey tied there, on which no one has ever sat. Untie it and bring it here. ³¹If anyone asks you, 'Why are you untying it?' say this: 'The Lord needs it.'"

³²So those who were sent left and found it just as He had told them. ³³As they were untying the young donkey, its owners said to them, "Why are you untying the donkey?"

³⁴"The Lord needs it," they said. ³⁵Then they brought it to Jesus, and after throwing their robes on the donkey, they helped Jesus get on it. ³⁶As He was going along, they were spreading their robes on the road. ³⁷Now He came near the path down the Mount of Olives, and the whole crowd of the disciples began to praise God joyfully with a loud voice for all the miracles they had seen:

> ³⁸   **The King who comes
>   in the name of the Lord**ᴶᴷ
>   **is the blessed One.**
>   Peace in heaven
>   and glory in the highest heaven!

ᴬ**19:8** Or *I give*   ᴮ**19:8** Or *I pay*   ᶜ**19:10** Or *save what was lost*   ᴰ**19:12** Lit *to receive for himself a kingdom* or *sovereignty*   ᴱ**19:13** = Gk coin worth 100 drachmas or about 100 days' wages   ᶠ**19:15** Lit *to receive for himself a kingdom* or *sovereignty*   ᴳ**19:17** Or *capable*   ᴴ**19:22** Lit *you out of your mouth*   ᴵ**19:27** Or *execute*   ᴶ**19:38** Luke substitutes "the King" for "He" in Ps 118:26.   ᴷ**19:38** Ps 118:26

³⁹ Some of the Pharisees from the crowd told Him, "Teacher, rebuke Your disciples."

⁴⁰ He answered, "I tell you, if they were to keep silent, the stones would cry out!"

⁴¹ As He approached and saw the city, He wept over it, ⁴² saying, "If you knew this day what would bring peace—but now it is hidden from your eyes. ⁴³ For the days will come on you when your enemies will build an embankment against you, surround you, and hem you in on every side. ⁴⁴ They will crush you and your children within you to the ground, and they will not leave one stone on another in you, because you did not recognize the time of your visitation."

⁴⁵ He went into the temple complex and began to throw out those who were selling,ᴬ ⁴⁶ and He said, "It is written, **My house will be a house of prayer,** but you have made it a **den of thieves!**"ᴮ

⁴⁷ Every day He was teaching in the temple complex. The chief priests, the scribes, and the leaders of the people were looking for a way to destroy Him, ⁴⁸ but they could not find a way to do it, because all the people were captivated by what they heard.ᶜ

20 One dayᴰ as He was teaching the people in the temple complex and proclaiming the good news, the chief priests and the scribes, with the elders, came up ² and said to Him: "Tell us, by what authority are You doing these things? Who is it who gave You this authority?"

³ He answered them, "I will also ask you a question. Tell Me, ⁴ was the baptism of John from heaven or from men?"

⁵ They discussed it among themselves: "If we say, 'From heaven,' He will say, 'Why didn't you believe him?' ⁶ But if we say, 'From men,' all the people will stone us, because they are convinced that John was a prophet."

⁷ So they answered that they did not know its origin.ᴱ

⁸ And Jesus said to them, "Neither will I tell you by what authority I do these things."

⁹ Then He began to tell the people this parable: "A man planted a vineyard, leased it to tenant farmers, and went away for a long time. ¹⁰ At harvest time he sent a slave to the farmers so that they might give him some fruit from the vineyard. But the farmers beat him and sent him away empty-handed. ¹¹ He sent yet another slave, but they beat that one too, treated him shamefully, and sent him away empty-handed. ¹² And he sent yet a third, but they wounded this one too and threw him out.

¹³ "Then the owner of the vineyard said, 'What should I do? I will send my beloved son. Perhapsᶠ they will respect him.'

¹⁴ "But when the tenant farmers saw him, they discussed it among themselves and said, 'This is the heir. Let's kill him, so the inheritance will be ours!' ¹⁵ So they threw him out of the vineyard and killed him.

"Therefore, what will the owner of the vineyard do to them? ¹⁶ He will come and destroy those farmers and give the vineyard to others."

But when they heard this they said, "No—never!"

¹⁷ But He looked at them and said, "Then what is the meaning of this Scripture:ᴳ

> The stone that the builders rejected—
> this has become the cornerstone?ᴴᴵ

¹⁸ Everyone who falls on that stone will be broken to pieces, and if it falls on anyone, it will grind him to powder!"

¹⁹ Then the scribes and the chief priests looked for a way to get their hands on Him that very hour, because they knew He had told this parable against them, but they feared the people.

²⁰ Theyᴶ watched closely and sent spies who pretended to be righteous,ᴷ so they could catch Him in what He said,ᴸ to hand Him over to the governor's rule and authority. ²¹ They questioned Him, "Teacher, we know that You speak and teach correctly, and You don't show partiality,ᴹ but teach truthfully the way of God. ²² Is it lawful for us to pay taxes to Caesar or not?"

²³ But detecting their craftiness, He said to them,ᴺ ²⁴ "Show Me a denarius. Whose image and inscription does it have?"

"Caesar's," they said.

²⁵ "Well then," He told them, "give back to Caesar the things that are Caesar's and to God the things that are God's."

ᴬ19:45 Other mss add *and buying in it*   ᴮ19:46 Is 56:7; Jr 7:11   ᶜ19:48 Lit *people hung on what they heard*   ᴰ20:1 Lit *It happened on one of the days*   ᴱ20:7 Or *know where it was from*   ᶠ20:13 Other mss add *when they see him*   ᴳ20:17 Lit *What then is this that is written*   ᴴ20:17 Lit *the head of the corner*   ᴵ20:17 Ps 118:22   ᴶ20:20 The scribes and chief priests of v. 19   ᴷ20:20 Or *upright*; that is, loyal to God's law   ᴸ20:20 Lit *catch Him in a word*   ᴹ20:21 Lit *You don't receive a face*   ᴺ20:23 Other mss add *"Why are you testing Me?*

²⁶They were not able to catch Him in what He said^A in public,^B and being amazed at His answer, they became silent.

²⁷Some of the Sadducees, who say there is no resurrection, came up and questioned Him: ²⁸"Teacher, Moses wrote for us that **if a man's brother** has a wife, and **dies childless, his brother should take the wife and produce offspring for his brother.**^C ²⁹Now there were seven brothers. The first took a wife and died without children. ³⁰Also the second^D ³¹and the third took her. In the same way, all seven died and left no children. ³²Finally, the woman died too. ³³In the resurrection, therefore, whose wife will the woman be? For all seven had married her."^E

³⁴Jesus told them, "The sons of this age marry and are given in marriage. ³⁵But those who are counted worthy to take part in that age and in the resurrection from the dead neither marry nor are given in marriage. ³⁶For they cannot die anymore, because they are like angels and are sons of God, since they are sons of the resurrection. ³⁷Moses even indicated in the passage about the burning bush that the dead are raised, where he calls the Lord the God of Abraham and the God of Isaac and the God of Jacob.^F ³⁸He is not God of the dead but of the living, because all are living to^G Him."

³⁹Some of the scribes answered, "Teacher, You have spoken well." ⁴⁰And they no longer dared to ask Him anything.

⁴¹Then He said to them, "How can they say that the Messiah is the Son of David? ⁴²For David himself says in the Book of Psalms:

> The Lord declared to my Lord,
> 'Sit at My right hand
> 43　until I make Your enemies
> 　　Your footstool.'^H

⁴⁴David calls Him 'Lord'; how then can the Messiah be his Son?"

⁴⁵While all the people were listening, He said to His disciples, ⁴⁶"Beware of the scribes, who want to go around in long robes and who love greetings in the marketplaces, the front seats in the synagogues, and the places of honor at banquets. ⁴⁷They devour widows'

houses and say long prayers just for show. These will receive greater punishment."^I

21 He looked up and saw the rich dropping their offerings into the temple treasury. ²He also saw a poor widow dropping in two tiny coins.^J ³"I tell you the truth," He said. "This poor widow has put in more than all of them. ⁴For all these people have put in gifts out of their surplus, but she out of her poverty has put in all she had to live on."

⁵As some were talking about the temple complex, how it was adorned with beautiful stones and gifts dedicated to God,^K He said, ⁶"These things that you see—the days will come when not one stone will be left on another that will not be thrown down!"

⁷"Teacher," they asked Him, "so when will these things be? And what will be the sign when these things are about to take place?"

⁸Then He said, "Watch out that you are not deceived. For many will come in My name, saying, 'I am He,' and, 'The time is near.' Don't follow them. ⁹When you hear of wars and rebellions,^L don't be alarmed. Indeed, these things must take place first, but the end won't come right away."

¹⁰Then He told them: "Nation will be raised up against nation, and kingdom against kingdom. ¹¹There will be violent earthquakes, and famines and plagues in various places, and there will be terrifying sights and great signs from heaven. ¹²But before all these things, they will lay their hands on you and persecute you. They will hand you over to the synagogues and prisons, and you will be brought before kings and governors because of My name. ¹³It will lead to an opportunity for you to witness.^M ¹⁴Therefore make up your minds^N not to prepare your defense ahead of time, ¹⁵for I will give you such words^O and a wisdom that none of your adversaries will be able to resist or contradict. ¹⁶You will even be betrayed by parents, brothers, relatives, and friends. They will kill some of you. ¹⁷You will be hated by everyone because of My name, ¹⁸but not a hair of your head will be lost. ¹⁹By your endurance gain^P your lives.

²⁰"When you see Jerusalem surrounded by armies, then recognize that its desolation has come near. ²¹Then those in Judea must flee

---

^A**20:26** Lit *catch Him in a word*　^B**20:26** Lit *in front of the people*　^C**20:28** Dt 25:5　^D**20:30** Other mss add *took her as wife, and he died without children*　^E**20:33** Lit *had her as wife*　^F**20:37** Ex 3:6,15　^G**20:38** Or *with*　^H**20:42-43** Ps 110:1　^I**20:47** Or *judgment*　^J**21:2** Lit *two lepta*; the *lepton* was the smallest and least valuable Gk coin in use.　^K**21:5** Gifts given to the temple in fulfillment of vows to God　^L**21:9** Or *insurrections*, or *revolutions*　^M**21:13** Lit *lead to a testimony for you*　^N**21:14** Lit *Therefore place* (determine) *in your hearts*　^O**21:15** Lit *you a mouth*　^P**21:19** Other mss read *endurance you will gain* to the mountains! Those inside the city^A must leave it, and those who are in the country must not enter it, [22]because these are days of vengeance to fulfill all the things that are written. [23]Woe to pregnant women and nursing mothers in those days, for there will be great distress in the land^B and wrath against this people. [24]They will fall by the edge of the sword and be led captive into all the nations, and Jerusalem will be trampled by the Gentiles^C until the times of the Gentiles are fulfilled.

[25]"Then there will be signs in the sun, moon, and stars; and there will be anguish on the earth among nations bewildered by the roaring sea and waves. [26]People will faint from fear and expectation of the things that are coming on the world, because the celestial powers will be shaken. [27]Then they will see the Son of Man coming in a cloud with power and great glory. [28]But when these things begin to take place, stand up and lift up your heads, because your redemption is near!"

[29]Then He told them a parable: "Look at the fig tree, and all the trees. [30]As soon as they put out leaves you can see for yourselves and recognize that summer is already near. [31]In the same way, when you see these things happening, recognize^D that the kingdom of God is near. [32]I assure you: This generation will certainly not pass away until all things take place. [33]Heaven and earth will pass away, but My words will never pass away.

[34]"Be on your guard, so that your minds are not dulled^E from carousing,^F drunkenness, and worries of life, or that day will come on you unexpectedly [35]like a trap. For it will come on all who live on the face of the whole earth. [36]But be alert at all times, praying that you may have strength^G to escape all these things that are going to take place and to stand before the Son of Man."

[37]During the day, He was teaching in the temple complex, but in the evening He would go out and spend the night on what is called the Mount of Olives. [38]Then all the people would come early in the morning to hear Him in the temple complex.

22 The Festival of Unleavened Bread, which is called Passover, was drawing near. [2]The chief priests and the scribes were looking for a way to put Him to death, because they were afraid of the people.

[3]Then Satan entered Judas, called Iscariot, who was numbered among the Twelve. [4]He went away and discussed with the chief priests and temple police how he could hand Him over to them. [5]They were glad and agreed to give him silver.^H [6]So he accepted the offer and started looking for a good opportunity to betray Him to them when the crowd was not present.

[7]Then the Day of Unleavened Bread came when the Passover lamb had to be sacrificed. [8]Jesus sent Peter and John, saying, "Go and prepare the Passover meal for us, so we can eat it."

[9]"Where do You want us to prepare it?" they asked Him.

[10]"Listen," He said to them, "when you've entered the city, a man carrying a water jug will meet you. Follow him into the house he enters. [11]Tell the owner of the house, 'The Teacher asks you, "Where is the guest room where I can eat the Passover with My disciples?"' [12]Then he will show you a large, furnished room upstairs. Make the preparations there."

[13]So they went and found it just as He had told them, and they prepared the Passover.

[14]When the hour came, He reclined at the table, and the apostles with Him. [15]Then He said to them, "I have fervently desired to eat this Passover with you before I suffer. [16]For I tell you, I will not eat it again^I until it is fulfilled in the kingdom of God." [17]Then He took a cup, and after giving thanks, He said, "Take this and share it among yourselves. [18]For I tell you, from now on I will not drink of the fruit of the vine until the kingdom of God comes."

[19]And He took bread, gave thanks, broke it, gave it to them, and said, "This is My body, which is given for you. Do this in remembrance of Me."

[20]In the same way He also took the cup after supper and said, "This cup is the new covenant established by My blood; it is shed for you.^J [21]But look, the hand of the one betraying Me is at the table with Me! [22]For the Son of Man will go away as it has been determined, but woe to that man by whom He is betrayed!"

²³ So they began to argue among themselves which of them it could be who was going to do this thing.

²⁴ Then a dispute also arose among them about who should be considered the greatest. ²⁵ But He said to them, "The kings of the Gentiles dominate them, and those who have authority over them are called^A 'Benefactors.'^B ²⁶ But it must not be like that among you. On the contrary, whoever is greatest among you must become like the youngest, and whoever leads, like the one serving. ²⁷ For who is greater, the one at the table or the one serving? Isn't it the one at the table? But I am among you as the One who serves. ²⁸ You are the ones who stood by Me in My trials. ²⁹ I bestow on you a kingdom, just as My Father bestowed one on Me, ³⁰ so that you may eat and drink at My table in My kingdom. And you will sit on thrones judging the 12 tribes of Israel.

³¹ "Simon, Simon,^C look out! Satan has asked to sift you^D like wheat. ³² But I have prayed for you^E that your faith may not fail. And you, when you have turned back, strengthen your brothers."

³³ "Lord," he told Him, "I'm ready to go with You both to prison and to death!"

³⁴ "I tell you, Peter," He said, "the rooster will not crow today until^F you deny three times that you know Me!"

³⁵ He also said to them, "When I sent you out without money-bag, traveling bag, or sandals, did you lack anything?"

"Not a thing," they said.

³⁶ Then He said to them, "But now, whoever has a money-bag should take it, and also a traveling bag. And whoever doesn't have a sword should sell his robe and buy one. ³⁷ For I tell you, what is written must be fulfilled in Me: **And He was counted among the outlaws.**^G Yes, what is written about Me is coming to its fulfillment."

³⁸ "Lord," they said, "look, here are two swords."

"Enough of that!"^H He told them.

³⁹ He went out and made His way as usual to the Mount of Olives, and the disciples followed Him. ⁴⁰ When He reached the place, He told them, "Pray that you may not enter into temptation." ⁴¹ Then He withdrew from them about a stone's throw, knelt down, and began to pray, ⁴² "Father, if You are willing, take this cup away from Me—nevertheless, not My will, but Yours, be done."

[⁴³ Then an angel from heaven appeared to Him, strengthening Him. ⁴⁴ Being in anguish, He prayed more fervently, and His sweat became like drops of blood falling to the ground.]^I ⁴⁵ When He got up from prayer and came to the disciples, He found them sleeping, exhausted from their grief.^J ⁴⁶ "Why are you sleeping?" He asked them. "Get up and pray, so that you won't enter into temptation."

⁴⁷ While He was still speaking, suddenly a mob was there, and one of the Twelve named Judas was leading them. He came near Jesus to kiss Him, ⁴⁸ but Jesus said to him, "Judas, are you betraying the Son of Man with a kiss?"

⁴⁹ When those around Him saw what was going to happen, they asked, "Lord, should we strike with the sword?" ⁵⁰ Then one of them struck the high priest's slave and cut off his right ear.

⁵¹ But Jesus responded, "No more of this!"^K And touching his ear, He healed him. ⁵² Then Jesus said to the chief priests, temple police, and the elders who had come for Him, "Have you come out with swords and clubs as if I were a criminal?^L ⁵³ Every day while I was with you in the temple complex, you never laid a hand on Me. But this is your hour—and the dominion of darkness."

⁵⁴ They seized Him, led Him away, and brought Him into the high priest's house. Meanwhile Peter was following at a distance. ⁵⁵ They lit a fire in the middle of the courtyard and sat down together, and Peter sat among them. ⁵⁶ When a servant saw him sitting in the firelight, and looked closely at him, she said, "This man was with Him too."

⁵⁷ But he denied it: "Woman, I don't know Him!"

⁵⁸ After a little while, someone else saw him and said, "You're one of them too!"

"Man, I am not!" Peter said.

⁵⁹ About an hour later, another kept insisting, "This man was certainly with Him, since he's also a Galilean."

⁶⁰ But Peter said, "Man, I don't know what you're talking about!" Immediately, while he

---

^A**22:25** Or *them call themselves*   ^B**22:25** Title of honor given to those who benefited the public good   ^C**22:31** Other mss read *Then the Lord said, "Simon, Simon*   ^D**22:31** In Gk, the word you is pl   ^E**22:32** In Gk, the word you is sg   ^F**22:34** Other mss read *before*   ^G**22:37** Is 53:12   ^H**22:38** Or *It is enough!*   ^I**22:43-44** Other mss omit bracketed text   ^J**22:45** Lit *sleeping from grief*   ^K**22:51** Lit *Permit as far as this*   ^L**22:52** Lit *as against a criminal* was still speaking, a rooster crowed. [61] Then the Lord turned and looked at Peter. So Peter remembered the word of the Lord, how He had said to him, "Before the rooster crows today, you will deny Me three times." [62] And he went outside and wept bitterly.

[63] The men who were holding Jesus started mocking and beating Him. [64] After blindfolding Him, they kept[A] asking, "Prophesy! Who hit You?" [65] And they were saying many other blasphemous things against Him.

[66] When daylight came, the elders[B] of the people, both the chief priests and the scribes, convened and brought Him before their Sanhedrin. [67] They said, "If You are the Messiah, tell us."

But He said to them, "If I do tell you, you will not believe. [68] And if I ask you, you will not answer. [69] But from now on, the Son of Man will be seated at the right hand of the Power of God."

[70] They all asked, "Are You, then, the Son of God?"

And He said to them, "You say that I am."

[71] "Why do we need any more testimony," they said, "since we've heard it ourselves from His mouth?"

23 Then their whole assembly rose up and brought Him before Pilate. [2] They began to accuse Him, saying, "We found this man subverting our nation, opposing payment of taxes to Caesar, and saying that He Himself is the Messiah, a King."

[3] So Pilate asked Him, "Are You the King of the Jews?"

He answered him, "You have said it."[C]

[4] Pilate then told the chief priests and the crowds, "I find no grounds for charging this man."

[5] But they kept insisting, "He stirs up the people, teaching throughout all Judea, from Galilee where He started even to here."

[6] When Pilate heard this,[D] he asked if the man was a Galilean. [7] Finding that He was under Herod's jurisdiction, he sent Him to Herod, who was also in Jerusalem during those days. [8] Herod was very glad to see Jesus; for a long time he had wanted to see Him because he had heard about Him and was hoping to see some miracle[E] performed by Him. [9] So he kept asking Him questions, but Jesus did not answer him. [10] The chief priests and the scribes stood by, vehemently accusing Him. [11] Then Herod, with his soldiers, treated Him with contempt, mocked Him, dressed Him in a brilliant robe, and sent Him back to Pilate. [12] That very day Herod and Pilate became friends.[F] Previously, they had been hostile toward each other.

[13] Pilate called together the chief priests, the leaders, and the people, [14] and said to them, "You have brought me this man as one who subverts the people. But in fact, after examining Him in your presence, I have found no grounds to charge this man with those things you accuse Him of. [15] Neither has Herod, because he sent Him back to us. Clearly, He has done nothing to deserve death. [16] Therefore, I will have Him whipped[G] and then release Him." [[17] For according to the festival he had to release someone to them.][H]

[18] Then they all cried out together, "Take this man away! Release Barabbas to us!" [19] (He had been thrown into prison for a rebellion that had taken place in the city, and for murder.)

[20] Pilate, wanting to release Jesus, addressed them again, [21] but they kept shouting, "Crucify! Crucify Him!"

[22] A third time he said to them, "Why? What has this man done wrong? I have found in Him no grounds for the death penalty. Therefore, I will have Him whipped and then release Him."

[23] But they kept up the pressure, demanding with loud voices that He be crucified. And their voices[I] won out. [24] So Pilate decided to grant their demand [25] and released the one they were asking for, who had been thrown into prison for rebellion and murder. But he handed Jesus over to their will.

[26] As they led Him away, they seized Simon, a Cyrenian, who was coming in from the country, and laid the cross on him to carry behind Jesus. [27] A large crowd of people followed Him, including women who were mourning and lamenting Him. [28] But turning to them, Jesus said, "Daughters of Jerusalem, do not weep for Me, but weep for yourselves and your children. [29] Look, the days are coming when they will say, 'The women without children, the wombs that never bore and the breasts that never nursed, are fortunate!' [30] Then they will

[A]22:64 Other mss add *striking Him on the face and*   [B]22:66 Or *council of elders*   [C]23:3 Or *That is true*; an affirmative oath   [D]23:6 Other mss read *heard "Galilee"*   [E]23:8 Or *sign*   [F]23:12 Lit *friends with one another*   [G]23:16 Gk *paideuo*; to discipline or "teach a lesson"; 1Kg 12:11,14 LXX; 2Ch 10:11,14; perhaps a way of referring to the Roman scourging; Lat *flagellatio*   [H]23:17 Other mss omit bracketed text   [I]23:23 Other mss add *and those of the chief priests*

begin to say to the mountains, 'Fall on us!' and
to the hills, 'Cover us!'[A] 31 For if they do these
things when the wood is green, what will happen when it is dry?"

32 Two others—criminals—were also led
away to be executed with Him. 33 When they
arrived at the place called The Skull, they crucified Him there, along with the criminals,
one on the right and one on the left. [34 Then
Jesus said, "Father, forgive them, because they
do not know what they are doing."][B] And they
divided His clothes and cast lots.

35 The people stood watching, and even the
leaders kept scoffing: "He saved others; let
Him save Himself if this is God's Messiah, the
Chosen One!" 36 The soldiers also mocked Him.
They came offering Him sour wine 37 and said,
"If You are the King of the Jews, save Yourself!"

38 An inscription was above Him:[C]

THIS IS
THE KING OF THE JEWS.

39 Then one of the criminals hanging there
began to yell insults at[D] Him: "Aren't You the
Messiah? Save Yourself and us!"

40 But the other answered, rebuking him:
"Don't you even fear God, since you are undergoing the same punishment? 41 We are
punished justly, because we're getting back
what we deserve for the things we did, but this
man has done nothing wrong." 42 Then he said,
"Jesus, remember me[E] when You come into
Your kingdom!"

43 And He said to him, "I assure you: Today
you will be with Me in paradise."

44 It was now about noon,[F] and darkness
came over the whole land[G] until three,[H] 45 because the sun's light failed.[I] The curtain of the
sanctuary was split down the middle. 46 And
Jesus called out with a loud voice, "Father, **into**
Your hands I entrust My spirit."[J] Saying this,
He breathed His last.

47 When the centurion saw what happened,
he began to glorify God, saying, "This man
really was righteous!" 48 All the crowds that
had gathered for this spectacle, when they saw
what had taken place, went home, striking
their chests.[K] 49 But all who knew Him, including the women who had followed Him from
Galilee, stood at a distance, watching these
things.

50 There was a good and righteous man
named Joseph, a member of the Sanhedrin,
51 who had not agreed with their plan and action. He was from Arimathea, a Judean town,
and was looking forward to the kingdom of
God. 52 He approached Pilate and asked for
Jesus' body. 53 Taking it down, he wrapped it
in fine linen and placed it in a tomb cut into
the rock, where no one had ever been placed.[L]
54 It was preparation day, and the Sabbath was
about to begin.[M] 55 The women who had come
with Him from Galilee followed along and ob-
served the tomb and how His body was placed.
56 Then they returned and prepared spices and
perfumes. And they rested on the Sabbath according to the commandment.

24 On the first day of the week, very early
in the morning, they[N] came to the
tomb, bringing the spices they had prepared.
2 They found the stone rolled away from the
tomb. 3 They went in but did not find the body
of the Lord Jesus. 4 While they were perplexed
about this, suddenly two men stood by them in
dazzling clothes. 5 So the women were terrified
and bowed down to the ground.[O]

"Why are you looking for the living among
the dead?" asked the men. 6 "He is not here,
but He has been resurrected! Remember how
He spoke to you when He was still in Galilee,
7 saying, 'The Son of Man must be betrayed
into the hands of sinful men, be crucified, and
rise on the third day'?" 8 And they remembered
His words.

9 Returning from the tomb, they reported all
these things to the Eleven and to all the rest.
10 Mary Magdalene, Joanna, Mary the mother of
James, and the other women with them were
telling the apostles these things. 11 But these
words seemed like nonsense to them, and they
did not believe the women. 12 Peter, however,
got up and ran to the tomb. When he stooped
to look in, he saw only the linen cloths.[P] So
he went home, amazed at what had happened.

13 Now that same day two of them were on
their way to a village called[Q] Emmaus, which
was about seven miles[R] from Jerusalem.
14 Together they were discussing everything
that had taken place. 15 And while they were

[A]**23:30** Hs 10:8 [B]**23:34** Other mss omit bracketed text [C]**23:38** Other mss add *written in Greek, Latin, and Hebrew letters* [D]**23:39** Or *began to blaspheme* [E]**23:42** Other mss add *Lord* [F]**23:44** Lit *about the sixth hour* [G]**23:44** Or *whole earth* [H]**23:44** Lit *the ninth hour* [I]**23:45** Other mss read *three, and the sun was darkened* [J]**23:46** Ps 31:5 [K]**23:48** = mourning [L]**23:53** Or *interred*, or *laid* [M]**23:54** Lit *was dawning*; not in the morning but at sundown Friday [N]**24:1** Other mss add *and other women with them* [O]**24:5** Lit *and inclined their faces to the ground* [P]**24:12** Other mss add *lying there* [Q]**24:13** Lit *village, which name is* [R]**24:13** Lit *about 60 stadia*; 1 *stadion* = 600 feet discussing and arguing, Jesus Himself came near and began to walk along with them. [16] But they[A] were prevented from recognizing Him. [17] Then He asked them, "What is this dispute that you're having[B] with each other as you are walking?" And they stopped walking and looked discouraged.

[18] The one named Cleopas answered Him, "Are You the only visitor in Jerusalem who doesn't know the things that happened there in these days?"

[19] "What things?" He asked them.

So they said to Him, "The things concerning Jesus the Nazarene, who was a Prophet powerful in action and speech before God and all the people, [20] and how our chief priests and leaders handed Him over to be sentenced to death, and they crucified Him. [21] But we were hoping that He was the One who was about to redeem Israel. Besides all this, it's the third day since these things happened. [22] Moreover, some women from our group astounded us. They arrived early at the tomb, [23] and when they didn't find His body, they came and reported that they had seen a vision of angels who said He was alive. [24] Some of those who were with us went to the tomb and found it just as the women had said, but they didn't see Him."

[25] He said to them, "How unwise and slow you are to believe in your hearts all that the prophets have spoken! [26] Didn't the Messiah have to suffer these things and enter into His glory?" [27] Then beginning with Moses and all the Prophets, He interpreted for them the things concerning Himself in all the Scriptures.

[28] They came near the village where they were going, and He gave the impression that He was going farther. [29] But they urged Him: "Stay with us, because it's almost evening, and now the day is almost over." So He went in to stay with them.

[30] It was as He reclined at the table with them that He took the bread, blessed and broke it, and gave it to them. [31] Then their eyes were opened, and they recognized Him, but He disappeared from their sight. [32] So they said to each other, "Weren't our hearts ablaze within us while He was talking with us on the road and explaining the Scriptures to us?" [33] That very hour they got up and returned to Jerusalem. They found the Eleven and those with them gathered together, [34] who said,[C] "The Lord has certainly been raised, and has appeared to Simon!" [35] Then they began to describe what had happened on the road and how He was made known to them in the breaking of the bread.

[36] And as they were saying these things, He Himself stood among them. He said to them, "Peace to you!" [37] But they were startled and terrified and thought they were seeing a ghost. [38] "Why are you troubled?" He asked them. "And why do doubts arise in your hearts? [39] Look at My hands and My feet, that it is I Myself! Touch Me and see, because a ghost does not have flesh and bones as you can see I have." [40] Having said this, He showed them His hands and feet. [41] But while they still were amazed and unbelieving because of their joy, He asked them, "Do you have anything here to eat?" [42] So they gave Him a piece of a broiled fish,[D] [43] and He took it and ate in their presence.

[44] Then He told them, "These are My words that I spoke to you while I was still with you—that everything written about Me in the Law of Moses, the Prophets, and the Psalms must be fulfilled." [45] Then He opened their minds to understand the Scriptures. [46] He also said to them, "This is what is written:[E] The Messiah would suffer and rise from the dead the third day, [47] and repentance for[F] forgiveness of sins would be proclaimed in His name to all the nations, beginning at Jerusalem. [48] You are witnesses of these things. [49] And look, I am sending you[G] what My Father promised. As for you, stay in the city[H] until you are empowered[I] from on high."

[50] Then He led them out as far as Bethany, and lifting up His hands He blessed them. [51] And while He was blessing them, He left them and was carried up into heaven. [52] After worshiping Him, they returned to Jerusalem with great joy. [53] And they were continually in the temple complex praising God.[J]

[A]24:16 Lit their eyes   [B]24:17 Lit What are these words that you are exchanging   [C]24:34 Gk is specific that this refers to the Eleven and those with them.   [D]24:42 Other mss add and some honeycomb   [E]24:46 Other mss add and thus it was necessary that   [F]24:47 Other mss read repentance and   [G]24:49 Lit upon you   [H]24:49 Other mss add of Jerusalem   [I]24:49 Lit clothed with power   [J]24:53 Other mss read praising and blessing God. Amen.